JOHN
of
THE CROSS

The Ascent to Joy

JOHN
of
THE CROSS

The Ascent to Joy

selected spiritual writings

introduced and edited by
Marc Foley, O.C.D.

New City Press

In gratitude to my dear friend
Sandra "Max Perkins" Gettings
for the many long hours that she spent in proofreading
this manuscript and for her many helpful suggestions
that gave clarity and unity to the text.

Published in the United States by
New City Press, 202 Cardinal Rd., Hyde Park, NY 12538
www.newcitypress.com
© New City Press 2002

Cover picture by Sr. Mary Grace, O.P.
Cover design by Nick Cianfarani

Library of Congress Cataloging-in-Publication Data:

 John of the Cross, Saint, 1542-1591.
   [Selections. English. 2002]
   The ascent of joy : selected spiritual writings / John of the Cross ; selected, annotated,
 and introduced by Marc Foley.
       p. cm.
   Includes bibliographical references.
     1. Spiritual life--Catholic Church. I. Foley, Marc, 1949- II. Title.

   BX2179 .J63 2002
   248.2'2--dc21   2002-25527

Printed in Canada

Contents

Translation and Abbreviations

All quotations are taken from *The Collected Works of St. John of the Cross*, translated by Kieran Kavanaugh O.C.D. and Otilio Rodriguez O.C.D., Washington, D.C.: ICS Publications, 1991.

The abbreviations to John's works are as follows:

A   *The Ascent of Mount Carmel*

N   *The Dark Night of the Soul*

C   *The Spiritual Canticle*

F   *The Living Flame of Love*

Pre   *The Precautions*

Co   *The Counsels*

S   *The Sayings of Light and Love*

L   *Letters*

P   *Poetry*

Regarding references to both *The Ascent of Mount Carmel* and *The Dark Night of the Soul*, the first number indicates the book; the second number refers to the chapter, and the third number to the paragraph. For example, A 2. 3. 4 refers to Book two, chapter three, paragraph four of *The Ascent of Mount Carmel*. In like manner, for *The Spiritual Canticle* and *The Living Flame of Love*, the first number refers to the stanza, and the second number to the paragraph. Thus, C 3. 4 is a reference to stanza three paragraph four of *The Spiritual Canticle*.

Introduction

Biographical Sketch[1]

Origins and Youth

In Greek mythology Eros (desire) was born of the union of Plenty and Poverty; so too was the great Spanish poet of desire and the dark night, Saint John of the Cross. One day on his travels from Toledo to Medina del Campo, a prosperous silk merchant named Gonzalo de Yepes stopped in Fontiveros, a small town midway between Madrid and Salamanca, and there he met a poor weaver named Catalina Alvarez. They fell in love, were married in 1529, and bore three sons: Francisco (b. 1530), Luis (b. between 1531–1541), and Juan (Saint John of the Cross, b. 1542). However, this was a shameful union in the eyes of Gonzalo's family, for he had crossed over a social divide and married beneath his rank. This egregious violation of a social taboo was costly; his family disinherited him.[2]

Beginning his new life penniless, Gonzalo learned the skill of weaving from Catalina, and together they lived in Fontiveros where they eked out a living for themselves and their growing family. A couple of years after John was born, his father became ill and died two years later. Desperate, Catalina traveled to Toledo with her children to beg help from her brother-in-law who was an archdeacon. She was hopeful that she would receive assistance from him because she thought that since he was a cleric, he would take pity on her plight. She was wrong. When

Catalina asked him if he would be willing to take one of her children into his house, he refused. With her hopes dashed, she traveled to Gálvez, a town located twenty-six miles southeast of Toledo, to seek assistance from Juan de Yepes, a medical doctor, who was an uncle of her children. He received them warmly.

Juan de Yepes offered to raise Francisco as his own son. Catalina was grateful and returned to Fontiveros, leaving Francisco behind. All seemed to be going well until the doctor's wife thwarted Francisco's education and began to treat him cruelly. When Catalina learned of this, she traveled to Gálvez and brought Francisco back home to Fontiveros, where he took up his mother's trade in order to help support the family. In spite of this assistance, a lack of work forced Catalina to move to Arévalo, a town located seventeen miles northeast of Fontiveros. The family lived there for four years. John was six at the time; his brother Francisco was eighteen. Luis may have died during this time or perhaps even earlier; biographers are uncertain.

We know hardly anything about John during the four years that he lived in Arévalo, except the impact that his older brother Francisco had upon him. Francisco's early years in Arévalo were those of a wild youth, but as the result of a spiritual conversion, he began to live a life of prayer marked by deeds of charity to the poor. Not only was Francisco a source of edification for John, but Francisco also became a second father to him. It is no wonder that John often said of Francisco, "He's the greatest gift I have in the world."

Shortly after Francisco's conversion, he married Ana Izquierda, a poor girl from Muriel, a small town near Arévalo. Francisco and Ana lived in the Yepes' household where Ana learned weaving from Catalina. In spite of the extra income that Ana's weaving provided, the Yepes family was forced to relocate because they were in financial straits. This time they moved to Medina del Campo, a commercial center, situated nineteen miles north of Arévalo. The move proved to be a good one. The family found more work there and settled in Medina del Campo, never to relocate again. Medina del Campo would be John's home for the next thirteen years. These years proved to be some of the most formative of his life. It was in Medina del Campo that John began his formal education, was introduced to ministry, grew into a man (from age nine to twenty-two), and discerned his vocation in life.

John received his primary education at the School of Doctrine, a school for orphans and the poor. He also worked as an acolyte and sacristan in the monastery of Augustinian nuns. In addition, he was employed as an orderly in a hospital that primarily treated patients with venereal disease. This hospital was the sixteenth century equivalent of a twenty-first century hospice for people dying of AIDS.

Don Alonso Alvarez, the administrator of the hospital, recognized John's intelligence and helped to finance his education at the recently founded Jesuit college in Medina del Campo. For four years, probably between 1559 and 1563, John studied Greek, Latin, and the humanities.

Vocation to Carmel

During his student years, John became acquainted with the Carmelites in Medina. The order attracted him because of its Marian and contemplative dimensions. In 1564 he entered the Carmelite novitiate in Medina and received the name of John of St. Matthias. The following year, he was sent to Salamanca to study philosophy and theology and was ordained a priest in 1567. However, he still was not settled in his vocation.

John was seriously considering joining the Carthusians because he felt a call to live a deeper life of prayer and solitude. However, the course of his life was about to change. When he went home to Medina to say his first Mass, he met Teresa of Avila. She told John of her new foundations in which the Carmelite ideal was being lived and that she was planning to expand this way of life to the friars. Teresa convinced John that he could find what he was looking for without leaving Carmel. John was enthusiastic about this prospect and said that he would help Teresa in this new venture on the condition that he would not have to wait too long.

The following year a dilapidated old farmhouse in the village of Duruelo, situated midway between Salamanca and Avila, became the first monastery of friars of the Teresian Reform. John and two other Carmelite friars formed the community. To symbolize this new phase of his life, John changed his name to John of the Cross.

John and the other two friars lived on in Duruelo until June 1570, when they moved to a larger facility in the neighboring village of Mancera in order to accommodate an influx of vocations. John was appointed the novice master at Mancera, but as the vocations continued to increase, they needed a separate house to serve as a novitiate. So toward the end of 1570, John was sent to Pastrana to help establish what would become the novitiate of the Reform. The following year, the Reform had a sufficient number of new members to warrant its own house of studies, which was founded in Alcalá in 1571. John was sent there to help establish this new student community and was appointed its rector.

Infighting and the Dark Night

In the same year, Teresa was ordered by Pedro Fernández, the papal visitator, to return to the Incarnation, the convent in which she first entered religious life. She was to assume the responsibilities of prioress. The nuns opposed this appointment, because they were resentful that someone not of their own choosing was being forced upon them. They were also fearful that Teresa would try to impose her reforms upon them. There were many problems in the convent at that time since the community was impoverished and full of factions.

Teresa needed help in this difficult situation, so she obtained permission to have John come to Avila to be the confessor and spiritual director for the nuns. For the next five years between 1572 and 1577, John lived in Avila as confessor to the nuns of the Incarnation and ministered to the many needs of the local church. These were good years for John; he was involved in ministries that he loved and was able to deepen his relationship with Teresa. However, all this would change in 1577.

During John's years in Avila, opposition to the Reform was growing. The Reform was becoming suspect among the Carmelite friars because of misunderstanding and political interference on the part of King Philip II. The Reform was initially approved under the condition that the number of Reformed monasteries be limited and also that no Reformed communities be established in the province of Andalusia. Due to the meddling of Phillip II, these stipulations were violated. This engendered fear that the Reform was spinning out of control.

It was within this context of jurisdictional disputes and confusion that many looked upon John as a threat. Not only was he regarded as one of the leaders of the Reform, but many non-Reformed friars resented him for accepting the post of confessor to the nuns of the Incarnation, a position traditionally reserved for a non-Reformed friar. The non-Reformed friars perceived the Reformed friars as encroaching upon their territory.

As a result, in December 1577, John's Carmelite brothers abducted him from his chaplain's quarters in Avila, took him to Toledo, and told him to renounce the Reform. If he refused, he would be considered a rebel and put into prison. John refused.

For the next nine months, John was imprisoned in a six-by-ten-foot cell with no outside window, in unsanitary conditions, with very little to eat or drink. It was under these wretched conditions that some of John's greatest poems were composed—*The Spiritual Canticle* (the first thirty-one verses), *Stanzas of the Soul that Rejoices in Knowing God Through Faith,* and the *Romances.*

The Escape

One dark night in the summer of 1578, John made a harrowing escape from his prison cell by lowering himself out of a window by means of two blankets tied together. He made his way to the Carmelite nuns in Toledo who took him in and secretly arranged to have him placed in a nearby hospital to recuperate from his ordeal. John remained undetected in the hospital for six weeks. He then traveled one hundred and eighty miles south to the Reform monastery in Almodóvar del Campo.

When John arrived at Almodóvar, the Reform friars (now known as the Discalced or "barefoot" friars, as distinct from the other Carmelite friars known as the Observants) were having a meeting at which they elected their own superiors. In addition, they sent representatives to Rome in order to iron out the misunderstandings that had arisen between the two groups and to ask permission from the Holy See to become an independent province. At this meeting, the friars appointed John vicar of the monastery of El Calvario in the southern province of Andalusia to replace one of the friars who went to Rome as a delegate.

For the next ten years, John lived in Andalusia where he served in various positions within the newly autonomous Discalced province (1580); he served as rector of the Discalced college in Baeza, confessor to the Carmelite nuns in Beas, prior of Granada, and vicar provincial of Andalusia. This position entailed extensive traveling; he made canonical visitations to all the houses of friars and nuns in Andalusia and was directly involved in the founding of seven new monasteries of friars. It was also during these ten years that John wrote his major prose works: *The Ascent of Mount Carmel, The Dark Night of the Soul, The Spiritual Canticle,* and *The Living Flame of Love.*

The ten years that John lived in Andalusia were not easy ones. He thirsted for silence and solitude, only to be burdened with the duties of administration. John often felt like an exile among the extroverted Andalusians, and he once wrote that he felt abandoned in a foreign land from the people that he loved the most; "abandonment is a steel file" (L 1). It was during his stay in Andalusia that his mother Catalina died.

When John returned to his native Castile in 1588, he was elected to two positions: prior of the monastery at Segovia and third counselor to Nicolas Doria, the vicar general of the Reform.

Final Months

While John was Doria's counselor, John opposed him on various issues. In consequence, Doria stripped John of all of his offices. Free of official responsibility, John volunteered to go to the foreign missions in Mexico. Doria reassigned John to La Peñuela in Andalusia to prepare for his departure for the New World. While John was at La Peñuela, there was an attempt to expel him from the Order. Fray Diego Evangelista, who was a general definitor at the time, falsely accused John of improprieties with the Carmelite nuns. Years before, John had corrected Diego when John was his superior. Diego never forgot this. So, out of resentment, he used the power of his office to try to gather evidence that would destroy John's reputation.

During this time, John became sick and was moved to the monastery of Ubeda for medical assistance. When he arrived, Prior Francisco Crisóstomo, who also held a grudge against John for a past reprimand, greeted him coldly. As John was dying, he apologized to Crisóstomo for being a burden on the community. Crisóstomo was deeply moved by John's holiness and begged his forgiveness. John died on December 14, 1591.

Approaching the Text

John had a hard life, but it did not make him hard. On the contrary, the poverty and deprivation of his childhood, his work with the sick, his years spent as a tireless administrator, his cruel imprisonment, and his final trials of being falsely accused and ill-treated at the hands of his brothers were the means of transforming John into a gentle, loving human being. This is not to say that the pain of his life was transformative by itself but rather the choices that he made in the face of his sufferings were redemptive.

From his earliest years, John learned that the choices we make in life shape the persons we become and that what we love, ultimately defines who we are. As John writes, ". . . love effects a likeness between the lover and the loved" (A 1. 4. 3). John knew this truth from the stories that he had heard about the marriage of his parents. It was in their sacrificial love for one another that he first discovered that true detachment consists in the willing-ness to sacrifice everything for the sake of being united with one's beloved. "Deny your desires and you will find what your heart longs for" (S 15).

It is not remarkable that detachment from worldly goods became one of the hallmarks of John's spirituality. However, what is remarkable is that his teaching on detachment is of such a positive nature. Often children who have been subjected to early deprivation not only become greedy and possessive as a means to assuage their fears of being destitute, but also begrudge others what they want and deprive them whenever possible. This was not the case with John.[3] When John was in positions of authority, he was always sensitive to the needs of his brothers. For example, when he was the rector of the college in Baeza, he purchased some property in the country so that the students would have a quiet refuge from the noise of the city. Also, as prior of various monasteries, John was sensitive to the dejection of his brothers. Whenever he perceived that they were downcast, he would take them out into the country for recreation in order to relieve their sadness since he had a sense of humor and a gift to make people laugh. Also, when his brothers were sick, he used his background in nursing to attend to their needs. He never administered authority harshly and once said of religious supe-riors who were strict with their subjects, "That we can also find among pagans." John believed that growing in holiness does not make a person harsh and aloof but gentle and approachable. This was true in John's case. All classes of people felt comfortable with John and frequently came to him for advice and confession. He once said, "The holier the confessor, the less fear one should have of him."

There was nothing glum about John or morose about his notion of self sacrifice. On the contrary, he considered true self sacrifice the path to a happy life. Perhaps John first learned this by witnessing the change that took place in Francisco's life after his conversion; he saw that a true change of heart does not result in a person becoming self absorbed in pious practices but in a joyous life spent in loving service of God and neighbor. Union with God through love is the goal of John's spirituality, but because he often wrote about the Cross as the *means* to union, his spirituality has acquired the reputation of being stern and stark. This is a gross misinterpretation.

Perhaps the best tool by which to interpret John's writings, which often *sound* harsh and even inhumane, is the way that he lived. For example, in *The Precautions* John writes that in order to free ourselves from the harm of the world, we should do the following:

> You should have an equal love for and an equal forgetfulness of all persons, whether relatives or not, and withdraw your heart from relatives as much as from others, and in some ways even more for fear that flesh and blood might be quickened by the natural love that is ever alive among kin, and must always be mortified for the sake of spiritual perfection.
>
> (Pre 5)

The tonality of this text *is* stark and offers us no concrete examples from daily life that would guide us to understanding. In consequence, John's teaching often becomes easy prey to misinterpretations and gross distortions. The above precaution should be interpreted through the lens of one of John's basic principles of spirituality that warns us against becoming enmeshed in any *disordered* relationship. The precaution is not speaking against the good and natural affection that we have toward family members. He is neither advocating the repression of our familial feelings nor isolation from our kith and kin. If John were advocating some dispassionate form of asceticism, then how can we reconcile his teaching with his life? For not only did John freely acknowledge his great affection for his family members, but when he moved to Duruelo, he brought Catalina,

Francisco, and his family with him to work and live in the monastery.

John is not an easy read for several reasons. He is not a very careful writer; he often contradicts himself and rarely nuances what he writes. He never gives any real life examples that would elucidate what he is trying to say. Also, John often writes in the language of Scholastic philosophy that is both dry and often unintelligible to the modern reader, and the tonality of his words are frequently stark, thus masking the gentle hand that held the pen.

John himself admitted that his style was "awkward" (A Prol. 8). This admission should not be interpreted as an expression of humility but of his experience. John was primarily a poet; poetry was the medium through which he communicated the depths of his inner life with God. Prose was not his "native tongue"; it was his second language in which he was not fluent. It was a language that tongue-tied his heart. Something of John's spirit was lost in the translation from poetry to prose, and the reader can only begin to recover it by becoming familiar with his verse.

The Poetry

John is considered one of the greatest, and by some critics, *the greatest* poet that Spain has ever produced. This is not due to the volume of his work, which is very meager. John's entire body of work consists of only eleven poems. The greatness of his poetry lies in his ability to articulate the inarticulable.

Saint Teresa wrote that "It is one grace to receive the Lord's favor; another, to understand which favor and grace it is; and a third, to know how to describe and explain it."[4] John was blessed with all three graces to a high degree. He was the recipient of deep mystical graces and endowed with the poetic genius that enabled him to express the graces that he received. Yet, in spite of this, John's poetry is a stammering in the face of The Holy, for his poems are attempts to do the impossible, namely to express the inexpressible.

> Who can describe in writing the understanding he
> [God] gives to loving souls in whom he dwells? And
> who can express with words the experience he
> imparts to them? Who, finally, can explain the desires
> he gives them? Certainly, no one can! *Not even they who*
> *receive these communications.*
>
> (C Prol. 1) (italic added)

Does this mean that John's mystical experiences are
completely incommunicable? By no means. What he communicated is not on a rational level but a deeply spiritual plane: "for
mystical wisdom, that comes through love," can only be understood by a pure and loving soul (C Prol. 2). And the vehicles
through which this wisdom finds voice are the symbols and
metaphors contained in John's poems.

> . . . these persons let *something* of their experience
> overflow in figures, comparisons and similitudes, and
> from the abundance of their spirit pour out secrets
> and mysteries rather than rational explanations.
>
> (C Prol. 1) (italic added)

Consequently, the reader must not approach John's poetry
with an analytical mind, for "if these similitudes are not read
with the simplicity of the spirit of knowledge and love they
contain, they will seem to be absurdities rather than reasonable
utterances . . ." (C Prol. 1). Rather, one must enter into John's
poetry with prayerful reverence not only because they are sacraments of his experience of The Holy but also because they have
the power to lead us into our own Holy of Holies. The images
contained in John's poetry are archetypical; they symbolize the
deepest and most universal experiences of our encounters with
God and thus have the capacity to resonate with the deepest
parts of our being. Like any living symbol, John's poetry can help
to clarify our own experience by imaging the unique contours
and configurations of our spiritual journey.

The Goal

The goal of the spiritual life, according to John, is union with God through love, a state of being in which the soul is so transformed that it "appears to be God" for "it is God by participation" (A 2. 5. 7).[5] In saying that the soul *is* God, John is stressing the utter oneness that exists in union, but the qualifier *by participation* retains the distinction between Creator and creature. The metaphor that John uses to capture both the unity and distinction between God and the soul in union is that of *interpenetration*. In union, John says that the soul is like crystal clear glass that has become completely illuminated by the Sun (God); the light of the Sun so permeates and saturates every molecule of the glass that they are indistinguishable though distinct.

Another image of interpenetration John uses to express the nature of union is fire (God) that so unites itself with a log of wood (the soul) that it "transforms the wood into itself and makes it as beautiful as it is itself" (N 2. 10. 1).

In union, the beauty of the lover and her Beloved are so one that they become mirror images of each other.

> That I be so transformed in your beauty that we may be alike in beauty, and both behold ourselves in your beauty, possessing then your very beauty; this, in such a way that each looking at the other may see in the other their own beauty, since both are your beauty alone, I being absorbed in your beauty; hence, I shall see in your beauty, and you will see me in your beauty, and I shall see myself in you in your beauty, and you will see yourself in me in your beauty; that I may resemble you in your beauty, and you resemble me in your beauty, and my beauty be your beauty and your beauty my beauty; wherefore I shall be you in your beauty, and you will be me in your beauty, because your very beauty will be my beauty; and thus we shall behold each other in your beauty.
>
> (C 36. 5)

The mutuality of giving and receiving that we see in this text is an echo of John's favorite scripture passage, John 17, which treats of the exchange of glory between the Father and the Son. He committed this passage to memory and would often sing it to his brothers when they were on the road together. This passage was at the core of John's spiritual vision because it spoke of the intimate union within the Trinity that was for him a symbol of intimacy that we are called to share with God; the path that leads us to this intimacy with God John calls the dark night.

The Spiritual Journey: The Dark Night

The phrase "the dark night of the soul" conjures up images of excruciating suffering that the soul must endure on its way to God. Even though the dark night includes such experiences, it is a far more encompassing concept for John; it is his main metaphor for the *whole* of the spiritual journey; it is John's way of speaking of God's transforming presence in our lives and our response to it.

The Ascent of Mount Carmel/The Dark Night of the Soul

John uses two terms throughout his works, "passive" and "active." They are not easy terms to grasp because they are fluid. For example, the term passive refers to the work that God accomplishes in the soul (A 1. 13. 1). In this sense, at every stage of the journey there is always a passive dimension to the purification process because God is always guiding the soul. However, there is a specific mode of purification that John calls passive in which the soul has to endure the purification that God is passively accomplishing within it.

Similarly, the term "active" refers to "what one can do" (A 1. 13. 1), or the soul's response to God's grace, but what the soul can do will change along the road. In the more "active" stages of the journey the soul is called to practice the virtues, whereas during the passive purifications the primary response is to endure the purification that God is accomplishing with it.

To begin to understand the "passive" and "active" dimensions of the spiritual journey as we experience them in daily life let us begin with a "definition" of the dark night. John writes:

> This dark night is an inflow of God into the soul, which purges it of its habitual ignorances and imperfections, natural and spiritual, and which the contemplatives call infused contemplation or mystical theology. Through this contemplation, God teaches the soul secretly and instructs it in the perfection of love without its doing anything or understanding how this happens.
>
> (N 2. 5. 1)

Let us examine some common experiences so that we can understand more clearly the interrelationship between the passive and active dimensions of the dark night. Think of a time when you were just about to say something, when the words were on the tip of your tongue, but something inside you said, "Don't!" At such moments, we are not conscious of any specific reason we should keep silent; nevertheless, we instinctively know that God wants us to be silent because it is the loving thing to do. This is an example of being instructed in love without our doing anything or understanding how it happened. The "active" component of the dark night in this example is our choice to remain silent.

As another example, recall a time during prayer when you became acutely aware of some fault in yourself that previously you had been blind to. This is God enlightening our habitual ignorance. Our "active" response to this knowledge is choosing to do those things that are necessary in order to change our behavior.

In these simple examples, we see John's paradigm of the spiritual life in its most basic form; it is a response to Presence, but since the presence of God is manifested in our lives in various ways and depths of intensity, our response will take on different forms.

The Active Night of the Senses

John calls the first passive/active "stage" of the dark night the "active night of the senses." It refers to a person's efforts to coop- erate with the ordinary means of grace to lead a regulated spiri- tual life (e.g., making time for prayer, spiritual reading, etc.), avoid occasions of sins, and to practice the virtues.

John says that God usually assists the efforts of souls during this stage by giving them emotional support in the form of conso- lation that makes prayer delightful and the exercise of virtue easy; he compares God to a nursing mother feeding her child.

> It should be known, then, that God nurtures and caresses the soul, after it has been resolutely converted to his service, like a loving mother who warms her child with the heat of her bosom, nurses it with good milk and tender food, and carries and caresses it in her arms. . . . The grace of God acts just as a loving mother by re-engendering in the soul new enthusiasm and fervor in the service of God. With no effort on the soul's part, this grace causes it to taste sweet and delectable milk and to experience intense satisfaction in the performance of spiritual exercises, because God is handling the breast of his tender love to the soul, just as if it were a delicate child.
>
> (N 1. 1. 2)[6]

The reason God does this is that these souls, which John calls "beginners," are still weak in the practice of virtue. Though they have made great progress in changing their behavior, the under- lying motive for the change has remained untouched. Just as they were attracted to the things of this world because of plea- sure, they are likewise drawn to the things of God because of pleasure.

Accordingly, God uses the pleasure of consolation to wean these souls away from harmful things and to enkindle in them a deeper love.

A love of pleasure, and attachment to it, usually fires the will toward the enjoyment of things that give pleasure. A more intense enkindling of another, better love (love of the soul's Bridegroom) is necessary for the vanquishing of the appetites and the denial of this pleasure. By finding satisfaction and strength in this love, it will have the courage and constancy to readily deny all other appetites.

(A 1. 14. 2)

For it is through the delight and satisfaction they experience in prayer that they have become detached from worldly things and have gained some spiritual strength in God.

(N 1. 8. 3)

This time of initial growth that is nurtured by God's consoling presence has been referred to as the "honeymoon" phase of the soul's relationship with God. Even though it is a time of real intimacy with God, there is also an element of unreality connected to it. These "beginners" have great fervor for the things of God, but their love has not yet been tested; spiritually they are still infants who operate on the pleasure principle for "their motivation in their spiritual works and exercises is the consolation and satisfaction they experience in them" (N 1. 1. 3). But when they have grown somewhat, God withdraws the sweet breast.

When God sees that they have grown a little, he weans them from the sweet breast so that they might be strengthened, lays aside their swaddling bands, and puts them down from his arms that they may grow accustomed to walking by themselves. This change is a surprise to them because everything seems to be functioning in reverse.

(N 1. 8. 3)

The Passive Night of the Senses
The Active Night of the Spirit

This withdrawing of God's palpable presence is the beginning of what John calls the "passive night of the senses." The soul no longer obtains pleasurable feelings from its meditations and thoughts about God; the practice of virtue becomes difficult and tedious, and everything related to the spiritual life feels empty and dry. God seems absent.

This is a time of great confusion and darkness. "Everything seems to be functioning in reverse" (N 1. 8. 3) because during the time of consolation, the soul had come to believe that feelings are the yardsticks for measuring spiritual growth: "The more deeply I feel the consoling presence of God, the closer I am to God." As a result of such an equation, "beginners" who now no longer experience these consolations, conclude that something must be wrong. Since they erroneously make a cause and effect connection between their efforts in prayer and consolation, they conclude that the problem must be that they are not trying hard enough. Therefore, they redouble their efforts at meditating and by sheer willpower try to regain their former fervor, but this only makes things worse; prayer becomes more dry and painful.

John says that the "beginners" may have completely misinterpreted their situation, namely, that the dryness and lack of consolation in prayer and the want of fervor for the things of God, may not be indications that something is *wrong* but signs that everything is *right*. Perhaps, what is happening, says John, is that God's inflow into the soul is now taking place on a deeper level. Thus, the soul can no longer experience God on the surface (in the senses) but on a more interior level (in the spirit).

Imagine the soul as an ocean. During the time of initial consolation, God is found on the surface, in the play of the waves and the dance of the sun upon the water. But during the passive night of the senses, God is on the bottom of the ocean where the water is deep and still. If the soul continues to seek God in the stimulation of the waves (in its reflections, thoughts, and meditations), it will remain frustrated. The soul must learn a new mode of prayer, namely, to sit quietly on the bottom of the ocean and "be content simply with a loving and peaceful attentiveness to God, and to live without the concern, without the effort, and without the desire to taste or feel him [God]" (N 1. 10. 4).

The question arises, how does a soul know that its lack of consolation is due to the work of God and is not the result of something else such as laxity? Here, John gives us "three signs" for discernment.

If the soul recognizes these three signs in itself, it can be confident that God is leading it into the passive night of the senses. If this is the case, it is not the time for the soul to be *thinking* about God but rather the time to simply *be* in God's presence. The passage quoted above contains more than a direction on how to be in God's presence during times of formal prayer; it hints at one of the major tasks on the spiritual journey that must be persevered for the rest of one's life: to walk by faith.

The Journey of Faith

What John means by faith is not an intellectual assent to the articles of the Creed but rather trust, the willingness to be led by God's Spirit, to attend and respond to the gentle, elusive Presence that is always present in the background of one's mind, or on the bottom of the ocean so to speak.

It is this attentive response to God's indwelling presence that is at the core of the "active night of the spirit" which runs parallel with the "passive night of the senses." This is not to say that faith was absent in the previous stage, but that now, it is a more fixed and constant part of a person's life. More and more the soul is becoming "passive," not in the sense of being inactive or inert, but rather in becoming more receptive and responsive to God's voice. In short, the soul is gradually relinquishing control over its life as it allows itself to be guided by God.

John says that a soul will ordinarily walk this path of faith for years and years, growing steadily in all of the virtues before the onset of the "passive night of the spirit."

The Passive Night of the Spirit

The passive night of the spirit can be seen as an intensification of the passive night of the senses in that it is the direct result of the inflow of God into the soul. However, in the night of the spirit, since God touches the innermost part of the soul, (the substance of the soul), the suffering is greater than in the previous purgation. One of the images that John uses in comparing the two purgations is that the night of the senses is like "cutting off the branches" of our sins and imperfections, and the night of the spirit is like "digging out the roots" (N 2. 2. 1).

In the passive night of the spirit, the roots of our sinfulness are laid bare. "Clearly beholding its impurity by means of this pure light . . ." (N 2. 5. 5) the soul becomes aware of its wretchedness and how shallow and mercenary is its love, and since it is so overwhelmed by what it sees, it cannot experience the Loving Light that manifests the inner darkness. In consequence, because the soul feels so unlovable, it believes that it is "abhorred not only by God but by every creature forever" (N 2. 7. 7). This is the most painful suffering of this night. The onslaught of God's presence in this passive night will come and go and vary in intensity according to what needs to be purified and the degree of sanctity to which God has deemed to raise a soul.

Finally, when we read about the passive night of the spirit as John presents in the second book of *The Dark Night,* one reason it is difficult to understand is that he does not situate it in daily experience; he does not put any flesh on it so to speak. As a result, it is easy to think that the night of the spirit is something that happens to us independent of what is going on in our day to day existence.

Take John's imprisonment as an example. Was this an experience of the dark night of the spirit? For John it was. Nevertheless, this does not mean that God "sent" this trial to him, or can we hold that being unjustly imprisoned is intrinsically a transforming experience, for many victims of injustice have grown embittered and spiteful because of their ordeal. What made John's trial redemptive was how he related to it; with God's grace he could forgive his brothers and endure his sufferings as a share in the cross of Christ. Likewise, any great trials, whether sickness, the death of a loved one, a deeply wounded childhood and its consequent impact upon our emotional life, etc., are examples of the raw material of a dark night experience.

Stages?

Can the different phases of the one dark night be considered sequential stages? The answer is *yes and no*. Yes, but only in a broad sense. John says that there are three characteristics by which God leads the soul "with order, gently, and according to the mode of the soul" (A 2. 17. 3). This means that God respects the order of things, and, thus, gradually detaches a soul from the least difficult thing to the most difficult.

However, the reader must not look at the different phases of the dark night in too linear a fashion. Yes, the "active night of the senses" is the "first stage" in that the main *emphasis* at the beginning of the journey is on active asceticism, but it is *not* a stage in the sense that asceticism is *left behind* after one advances to the "next stage." It would be naive to think that one can ever completely dispense with asceticism characteristic of the "active night of the senses" anywhere along the journey. In fact, the practice of traditional forms of asceticism may become crucial during the "passive night of the spirit" in order to guard the soul against compensating for the void that it is experiencing by inordinately indulging its sensual appetites.

When we say that a person is *in* a particular stage of the dark night, we mean that a specific mode of God's presence and the soul's corresponding response that are characteristic of that stage are the ones that are *most prominent*. It does not mean that the other modes of the dark night are absent. Life is too complex and lived on too many levels simultaneously to afford such a simplistic paradigm of spiritual growth. In real life, the different phases of the dark night overlap and run parallel to one another.

Other Major Prose Works: The Spiritual Canticle

The Spiritual Canticle is John's commentary on his poem of the same name. The main theme of this work, which is presented in the form of a dialogue between two lovers, is the Bride's (soul) desire for her Bridegroom (God) who has "wounded" her with love. It is this love or desire for her Beloved that impels her to abandon all things in order to go out in search of him (stanzas 1–13). This is a basic theme in John's writings, namely, that our desire for God, which is actually an experience of God, is what detaches us from our inordinate desires that keep us from God.

In stanzas fourteen and fifteen, the Bride sings of her joy of being reunited with her Beloved (the spiritual espousal), but since this union with him is not complete, her restlessness soon returns (stanzas 16–21). It is only in stanzas twenty-two through twenty-five that the Bride's desire is quelled as she enters into the spiritual marriage; yet, stanzas thirty-six through forty record the Bride's desire to contemplate the vastness of her Beloved's beauty that will only be revealed in eternity.

Thus, the work ends where it began with desire. In its broadest outline, *The Spiritual Canticle* is in the shape of an ever widening gyre that spirals upwards from desire to desire satisfied, circling back again to desire, each time growing in intensity. This spiraling between desire and desire satisfied speaks of two important themes that appear in John's writings.

The first is indicative of an archetypical pattern in the transformation process: that periods of darkness are followed by intervals of light. John compares the work of God in the dark night to that of a blacksmith. When God's purgative presence is at work transforming the soul, it is like those times that the iron is immersed in the forge; the soul is in darkness and feels that God is absent. However, there are times when the blacksmith draws the iron out of the fire to examine how his work is proceeding. Then the iron glows. At these moments, the soul feels that God is present once again, for it "is able to perceive that good it was unaware of while the work was proceeding" (N 2. 10. 6).

The second thing that the spiraling from desire to desire satisfied speaks of is that there are primarily two ways that we experience God in life. The first, as we would expect, is in those moments when we *feel* God's presence. The second is in our desire for God, that is, when we feel that God is absent. In other words, what we long for is *in the longing.*

Finally, what is central to *The Spiritual Canticle* (and *The Living Flame of Love*) is John's presentation of God as one who loves us passionately and who seeks and desires to be united with us more than we seek and desire to be united with God. In fact, what the Bride labels as *her* desire for God is ultimately revealed as *God's* desire for her; "it should be known that if anyone is seeking God, the Beloved is seeking that person much more" (F 3. 28).

The Living Flame of Love

The Living Flame of Love is the most mystical of John's writings; it describes a soul *within* the state of union that sings of the fire of God's love that so touches the substance of her being and transforms her *into* God that "all the movements of this soul are divine" (F 1. 9). The central image of union in the *The Living Flame of Love* is a log (the soul) that is so united with fire (God) that it has become transformed into a glowing, pulsating ember; the flame that springs up from the log (a living flame) is the activity of the Holy Spirit who is so united with the activity of the soul that the soul loves with the love of God. Thus, the acts of the soul springing from the state of union are "more meritorious and valuable than all the deeds a person may have performed in the whole of life without this transformation" (F 1. 3). In short, the soul has become an incarnation of God. The depth, beauty, and tonality of John's descriptions of a soul in union in this work are comparable to what Dante has written of the blessed in the *Paradiso.*

However, frequently John digresses from this main topic to deal at length with other subjects such as the role of spiritual directors.

Minor Works: The Counsels and The Precautions

Both of these works are a series of essential disciplines to be practiced and warnings to be heeded by anyone serious about growing in the spiritual life. *The Precautions* consists of nine pieces of advice on how to avoid falling prey to the three major enemies of the soul: the world, the flesh, and the devil. *The Counsels* are similar but focus on other areas in the spiritual life: resignation, being constant in the practice of virtue, the practice of solitude, and mortification.

Like all of John's works, although the tonality of *The Counsels* and *The Precautions* may sound stark, their fruits are positive: "holy recollection and spiritual silence, nakedness, and poverty of spirit, where one enjoys the peaceful comfort of the Holy Spirit." (Pre 1)

When Thomas Merton was preparing to make his solemn profession he read both *The Counsels* and *The Precautions.* He wrote of them:

> I prepared for profession by praying over the *Cautions* and *Counsels* of Saint John of the Cross. For the rest of my religious life I would like, by keeping these *Counsels,* to dispose myself for the work God wants to do in me to which I am completely consecrated. . . . They seem to me to be the most detailed and concrete and practical set of rules for arriving at religious perfection that I have ever seen.[7]

The Sayings of Light and Love

These maxims are nuggets of spiritual wisdom comparable to those of Zen masters or the Desert writers of the fourth century. They are distillations of John's teachings, many of which he wrote for his penitents as aids to reflection and spiritual counsel.

Letters

John wrote many letters throughout his life, but only thirty-three of them (eight of which are fragments) have survived. In the final months of John's life, Carmelite nuns destroyed a number of his letters; they were afraid that they would fall into the hands of Diego Evangelista who would twist the meaning of what John wrote and use them as evidence to prove that John had inordinate affection for some of the nuns.

But those that have survived give us a glimpse into a very compassionate man who administered spiritual advice with great affection and sensitivity; his letters are warm and offer the substance of his teaching minus the heavy philosophical language characteristic of his major tomes. After his poetry, John's letters are perhaps the best place to begin reading his works.

Conclusion

Frequently, the popular mind has regarded John's spirituality as forbidding and even inhumane. This image is partly due to the stark style of his writing, but perhaps the real reason for the negative reaction to his work is that John presents us with a spirituality of substance that lays bare the core of the gospel, namely, that we can only come to share in the Resurrection by walking the way of the Cross. This is something that very few of us want to hear, and John knew it. He wrote:

> But if some people still find difficulty in understanding this doctrine, it will be due to my deficient knowledge and awkward style, for the doctrine itself is good and very necessary. But I am inclined to believe that, even if it were presented with greater accuracy and polish, only a few would profit in it, because we are not writing on moral and pleasing

topics addressed to the kind of spiritual people who
like to approach God along sweet and satisfying paths.
We are presenting a substantial and solid doctrine for
all those who desire to reach this nakedness of spirit.

(A Prol. 8)

However, John's writings are *not* for the few; as a Doctor of the
Church, John offers to all the faithful a sure guide to holiness.
Perhaps the most valuable insight that runs throughout John's
writings is that he teaches us how to interpret our experience
from a spiritual perspective. For example, he helps us to discern
that when we *feel* that God is absent, that our longing for God
may be an experience of the God for whom we long; similarly,
when the darkness we see within overwhelms us, this is the
result of God's loving light shining brightly in our lives. John
gives us the assurance that when we believe that "everything
seems to be functioning in reverse" (N 1. 8. 3), that things are
going forward.

The spiritual path that John marks out will often lead us
through many dark nights. This is reality; it is not John's inven-
tion. But John reassures us that the God who accompanies us on
our way is a God of love.

Marc Foley, O.C.D.
On the Feast of Saint Kaitlin
(October 30)

Notes

1. I am indebted to many sources for the biographical information in this
introduction. Chief among them is Kieran Kavanaugh's excellent introduc-
tions and notes from his translation of *The Collected Works of St. John of the
Cross* (Washington, DC: ICS Publications, 1991). I have also relied heavily on
various articles that appear in *God Speaks in the Night: The Life, Times, and
Teaching of St. John of the Cross,* edited by Federico Ruiz (Washington, DC: ICS
Publications, 1991).

2. Another possible reason why Gonzalo's family disowned him was that his family were Jewish converts, and Catalina was thought not to be *limieza de sangre* (purity of blood); she was suspected of being Moorish. This frightened Gonzalo's family. If the Inquisition began to delve into Catalina's background, might their prodding not lead to an investigation of their own background?

3. Karen Horney, *The Neurotic Personality of our Times* (New York: W.W, Norton Publishing Co., 1964), 145–54.

4. Teresa of Avila, *"The Book of Her Life,"* in *The Collected Works of St. Teresa of Avila,* vol. 1, trans. Otilio Rodriguez O.C.D. and Kieran Kavanaugh O.C.D. (Washington, DC: ICS Publications, 1980), 154.

5. I use the word "soul" in the way that John uses it most frequently in his writings, to designate the whole of human nature. In general, John's use of the word soul (alma) is roughly equivalent to the word "person" in English.

6. Also see the following passages where John compares God to a nursing mother: Cf. A 2. 14. 3; 2. 17. 6–7; 3. 28. 7.

7. Thomas Merton, *The Sign of Jonas* (New York: Harcourt, Brace and Company, 1953), 32.

The Poetry

The three poems in this section are John's most famous ones: *The Spiritual Canticle, The Dark Night,* and *The Living Flame of Love.* Even though he used them as the basis of his major commentaries, it is important to keep in mind that the poems were composed not only prior to his commentaries but independent of them. John did not plan to write commentaries on his poetry; they were later developments that arose as the result of requests.

These facts are important to remember as we read John's poetry, lest our knowledge of what John says in his commentaries "contaminates" our hearing his poetry fresh. To approach John's poetry with preconceived ideas of what the images symbolize is to put our imagination in an allegorical straightjacket.

Our Western mind tends to approach poetry from an *author-centered* prospective, it poses questions such as "What did the author mean, etc.?" It is concerned with collecting background information about the composition of the poem. While such an approach may eventually enrich our understanding of a poem, in this author's opinion, it is not the best way to approach a poem for the *first* time. I suggest that the reader take a *text-centered* approach to John's poetry; simply let the poems speak to your heart and your own experience.[1]

The Spiritual Canticle

During his imprisonment, John wrote most of *The Spiritual Canticle*. The
poem is based primarily upon the *Song of Songs* that John knew by heart
and was a favorite vehicle for medieval saints and mystics to help
verbalize their experience of God; in it they found images of human
love, intimacy, and surrender that best expressed their experience of
union with the Divine.[2] Evelyn Underhill writes:

> It has been said that the constant use of such imagery [of
> human love and marriage] by Christian mystics of the
> mediaeval period is traceable to the popularity of the Song
> of Songs, regarded as the allegory of the spiritual life. I think
> that the truth lies in the opposite statement: namely, that
> the mystic loved the Song of Songs because he there saw
> reflected, as in a mirror, the most secret experiences of the
> soul. The sense of a desire that was insatiable . . . that it
> could only be compared with the constant link of human
> love . . . that august passion in which the merely human
> draws nearest to the divine.[3]

We can read John's poem on different levels. On a spiritual plane it is
about the soul's insatiable desire for the Infinite. Such a spiritual
reading of the poem is valid based upon John's life and his commentary
on the poem, but perhaps this is not the first place to begin. Should we
not read it first for what it is, a love poem? Perhaps this was John's
intention, for the original title that John gave the poem was *Canciones
entre el alma y el esposo* (Stanzas between the soul and its Bridegroom).
On the literal level, the poem is an expression of love between a man and
a woman; God is never even mentioned in the poem. It was only forty
years after John's death that editors revised the title to *The Spiritual
Canticle between the Soul and Christ the Bridegroom*; eventually, they short-
ened the title to *The Spiritual Canticle*.

It is important to stay rooted in the literal level of a text because it keeps
us grounded in human experience that is the doorway through which
we access the text's deeper layers of meaning. Just as Thomas Aquinas
said that all the different "senses" of Scripture (e.g., allegorical, spiritual, etc.) are based upon and presuppose the literal level, the same can
be said of John's poetry.

The Spiritual Canticle[4]

Stanzas between the Soul and the Bridegroom

Bride
1. Where have you hidden,
Beloved, and left me moaning?
You fled like the stag
after wounding me;
I went out calling you, but you were gone.

2. Shepherds, you who go up through the sheepfolds to the hill,
if by chance you see
him I love most,
tell him I am sick, I suffer, and I die.

3. Seeking my Love
I will head for the mountains and for watersides;
I will not gather flowers,
nor fear wild beasts;
I will go beyond strong men and frontiers.

4. O woods and thickets,
planted by the hand of my Beloved!
O green meadow,
coated, bright, with flowers,
tell me, has he passed by you?

5. Pouring out a thousand graces,
he passed these groves in haste;
and having looked at them,
with his image alone,
clothed them in beauty.

6. Ah, who has the power to heal me?
Now wholly surrender yourself!
Do not send me
any more messengers,
they cannot tell me what I must hear.

7. All who are free
tell me a thousand graceful things of you;
and wound me more
and leave me dying
of, ah, I don't know what's behind their stammering.

8. How do you endure
O life, not living where you live,
and being brought near death
by the arrows you receive
from that which you conceive of your Beloved?

9. Why, since you wounded
this heart, don't you heal it?
And why, since you stole it from me,
do you leave it so,
and fail to carry off what you have stolen?

10. Extinguish these miseries,
since no one else can stamp them out;
and may my eyes behold you,
because you are their light,
and I would open them to you alone.

11. Reveal your presence,
and may the vision of your beauty be my death;
for the sickness of love
is not cured
except by your very presence and image.

12. O spring like crystal!
If only, on your silvered-over faces,
you would suddenly form
the eyes I have desired,
which I bear sketched deep within my heart.

13. Withdraw them, Beloved,
I am taking flight!

Bridegroom
Return, dove,
the wounded stag
is in sight on the hill,
cooled by the breeze of your flight.

Bride
14. My Beloved, the mountains,
and lonely wooded valleys,
strange islands,
and resounding rivers,
the whistling of love-stirring breezes,

15. the tranquil night
at the time of the rising dawn,
silent music,
sounding solitude,
the supper that refreshes, and deepens love.

16. Catch us the foxes,
for our vineyard is now in flower,
while we fashion a cone of roses
intricate as the pine's;
and let no one appear on the hill.

17. Be still, deadening north wind;
south wind, come, you that waken love,
breathe through my garden,
let its fragrance flow,
and the Beloved will feed amid the flowers.

18. You girls of Judea,
while among flowers and roses
the amber spreads its perfume,
stay away, there on the outskirts:
do not so much as seek to touch our thresholds.

19. Hide yourself, my love;
turn your face toward the mountains,

and do not speak;
but look at those companions
going with her through strange islands.[5]

Bridegroom
20. Swift-winged birds,
lions, stags, and leaping roes,
mountains, lowlands, and river banks,
waters, winds, and ardors,
watching fears of night:

21. By the pleasant lyres
and the siren's song, I conjure you
to cease your anger
and do not touch the wall,
that the bride may sleep in deeper peace.

22. The bride has entered
the sweet garden of her desire,
and she rests in delight,
laying her neck
on the gentle arms of her Beloved.

23. Beneath the apple tree:
there I took you for my own,
there I offered you my hand,
and restored you,
where your mother was corrupted.

Bride
24. Our bed is in flower,
bound round with linking dens of lions,
hung with purple,
built up in peace,
and crowned with a thousand shields of gold.

25. Following your footprints
maidens run along the way;
the touch of a spark,

the spiced wine,
cause flowings in them from the balsam of God.

26. In the inner wine cellar
I drank of my Beloved, and, when I went aboard
through all this valley
I no longer knew anything,
and lost the herd that I was following.

27. There he gave me his breast;
there he taught me a sweet and living knowledge;
and I gave myself to him,
keeping nothing back;
there I promised to be his bride.

28. Now I occupy my soul
and all my energy in his service;
I no longer tend the herd,
nor have I any other work
now that my every act is love.

29. If, then, I am no longer
seen or found on the common,
you will say that I am lost;
that, stricken by love,
I lost myself, and was found.

30. With flowers and emeralds
chosen on cool mornings
we shall weave garlands
flowering in your love,
and bound with one hair of mine.

31. You considered
that one hair fluttering at my neck;
you gazed at it upon my neck
and it captivated you;
and one of my eyes wounded you.

32. When you looked at me
your eyes imprinted your grace in me;
for this you loved me ardently;
and thus my eyes deserved
to adore what they beheld in you.

33. Do not despise me;
for if, before, you found me dark,
now truly you can look at me
since you have looked
and left in me grace and beauty.

Bridegroom
34. The small white dove
has returned to the ark with an olive branch;
and now the turtledove
has found its longed-for mate
by the green river banks.

35. She lived in solitude,
and now in solitude has built her nest;
and in solitude he guides her,
he alone, who also bears
in solitude the wound of love.

Bride
36. Let us rejoice, Beloved,
and let us go forth to behold ourselves in your beauty,
to the mountain and to the hill,
to where the pure water flows,
and further, deep into the thicket.[6]

37. And then we will go on
to the high caverns in the rock
which are so well concealed;
there we shall enter
and taste the fresh juice of the pomegranates.

38. There you will show me
what my soul has been seeking,
and then you will give me,
you, my life, will give me there
what you gave me on that other day:

39. the breathing of the air,
the song of the sweet nightingale,
the grove and its living beauty
in the serene night,
with a flame that is consuming and painless.

40. No one looked at her,
nor did Aminadab appear;
the siege was still;
and the cavalry,
at the sight of the waters, descended.

The Dark Night

The tonality of this poem is much different from that of *The Spiritual Canticle;* we do not hear any anguished longing or cry of pain from the protagonist. In fact, *The Dark Night* does not seem to contain a "dark night" experience at all. It is the story of a passionate young woman who sneaks out of her house one night while everyone is asleep and spends a night of love with her Beloved.

One of the reasons why the two poems differ in tonality is the circumstances in which John wrote them. John composed *The Spiritual Canticle* while he was in jail; it reflects not only the anguish of his imprisonment but also the pain of inner transformation. On the other hand, John wrote *The Dark Night* after his escape, perhaps during his recuperation; it is a backward glance and a song of praise and thanksgiving about what Amazing Grace has done in him. It sings of both his escape from the prison of Toledo and the inner transformation that has united him with God. It is "A song of the soul's happiness in *having passed through* the dark night of faith, in nakedness and purgation, to union with God" (Italic added) (A. Stanzas). The poem invites the reader to reflect upon what grace has done in his or her own life.[7]

The Dark Night

1. One dark night,
fired with love's urgent longings
—ah, the sheer grace!—
I went out unseen,
my house being now all stilled.

2. In darkness and secure,
by the secret ladder, disguised,
—ah, the sheer grace!—
in darkness and concealment,
my house being now all stilled.

3. On that glad night,
in secret, for no one saw me,
nor did I look at anything,

with no other light or guide
than the one that burned in my heart.

4. This guided me
more surely than the light of noon
to where he was awaiting me
—him I knew so well—
there in a place where no one appeared.

5. O guiding night!
O night more lovely than the dawn!
O night that has united
the Lover with his beloved,
transforming the beloved in her Lover.

6. Upon my flowering breast
which I kept wholly for him alone,
there he lay sleeping,
and I caressing him
there in a breeze from the fanning cedars.

7. When the breeze blew from the turret,
as I parted his hair,
it wounded my neck
with its gentle hand,
suspending all my senses.

8. I abandoned and forgot myself,
laying my face on my Beloved;
all things ceased; I went out from myself,
leaving my cares
forgotten among the lilies.

The Living Flame of Love

As in the previous two poems, *The Living Flame of Love* is erotic in its symbolism. Just as John's commentary speaks of the most sublime union that can exist here on earth between God and a soul, so does the poem echo the climactic union of a man and women in the act of making love; it "is an intimate description of sexual union and tenderness," writes Barnstone.[8]

In the first stanza the lover asks that her beloved, who is wounding her with love in her deepest center, consummate his love and "tear through the veil of this sweet encounter!" This line has been translated various ways to express its erotic connotation: "And for our sweet encounter tear the robe!" (Campbell), "Break the membrane of our sweet union" (Barnstone).

In stanzas two and three there is a poverty of verbs but an overabundance of "O's" and "How's" to express the ecstasy of the encounter.

Stanza four is similar to the last stanza of *The Spiritual Canticle;* there are no fireworks or grand finales but rather a deep peace of being at home with oneself and one's Beloved. Stanza four expresses the "immense tranquility" (F 4. 15) of "one who on awakening breathes deeply" (F 4. 3). The stanza is not anticlimactic but post climactic.

The Living Flame of Love

1. O living flame of love
that tenderly wounds my soul
in its deepest center! Since
now you are not oppressive,
now consummate! If it be your will:
tear through the veil of this sweet encounter!

2. O sweet cautery,
O delightful wound!
O gentle hand! O delicate touch
that tastes of eternal life
and pays every debt!
In killing you changed death to life.

3. O lamps of fire!
in whose splendors
the deep caverns of feeling,
once obscure and blind,
now give forth, so rarely, so exquisitely,
both warmth and light to their Beloved.

4. How gentle and lovingly
you wake in my heart,
where in secret you dwell alone;
and in your sweet breathing,
filled with good and glory,
how tenderly you swell my heart with love.

Notes

1. For a good treatment of the difference between an "author-centered" and a "reader-centered" approach to the *The Spiritual Canticle* see *Canciones Entre El Alma Y El Esposo of Juan De La Cruz: A Hermeneutical Interpretation* (San Francisco: Catholic Scholars Print, 1966), esp. 1–10.

2. John's poem may also have been influenced by the popular love poetry of his time which centered around the theme of unrequited love and which took the form of a dialogue between lovers. He grew up in a culture in which it was common practice to use secular songs and poems to celebrate divine love. See George Tavard, *Poetry and Contemplation in St. John of the Cross* (Athens, OH: Ohio University Press, 1988), 1-13.

3. Evelyn Underhill, *Mysticism* (New York: E. P. Dutton & Co. Inc, 1961), 137.

4. There are two redactions of this poem; they differ from one another in both the number and sequence of stanzas. The second redaction—which is the poem that follows—has an additional stanza (stanza eleven). John revised the poem as he revised his commentary on the poem.

5. There is evidence to suggest that this stanza was inspired by a verse from a popular song that John heard a boy singing outside his prison cell. See Colin Thompson's *The Poet and the Mystic: A Study of the Cantico Espiritual of San Juan de la Cruz* (Oxford: Oxford University Press, 1977), 29.

6. There is a story that says that John once asked a Carmelite nun in Beas the manner of her prayer. When she responded that it consisted of beholding God's beauty and rejoicing that God possessed it, John was so moved by

her answer that he pondered the beauty of God for several days afterward, and out of his reflections, he wrote the last stanzas of the *The Spiritual Canticle,* beginning with the line, "Let us rejoice, Beloved, and let us go forth to behold ourselves in your beauty." The accuracy of this story is questioned by some scholars. See Thompson, *The Poet and the Mystic,* 29-30.

7. It seems that it is important to John that the reader is conscious of the vantage point of the soul that sings this song for John also stresses this at the beginning of *The Dark Night of the Soul.* "Before embarking on the explanation of these stanzas, we should remember that the soul recites them when it *has already reached* the state of perfection" (italic added) (N. Prologue to the Reader).

8. Willis Barnstone, trans., *The Poems of Saint John of the Cross* (New York: New Directions Books, 1972), 32. occurrences.

The Goal: Union with God

John distinguishes three ways that God is united with the soul: by essence (substantially), by grace, and by spiritual affection (C 11. 3) that may also be seen as three degrees of the soul's awareness of God's presence.

The first way that God is united with the soul is by his essence, that is, the Divine Presence that sustains us in existence. This "sustaining" presence is neither some impersonal mode of existence, nor does it mean that God is only partially present to the soul by a single attribute (e.g., power). By essence, God is fully united with the soul by means of love, mercy, wisdom, goodness, etc. (F 3. 2). Substantial union, that is, the result of God's presence by essence, is one of great intimacy between God and the soul, for to say that we are *creatio ex nihilo,* created out of nothing, means that *nothing* stands between us and God's loving presence; it says that God so completely permeates and saturates our being that we cannot experience anything apart from God. Consequent upon this divine intimacy, there exists in the soul a permanent intimation of God's presence as mystery that is apprehended in all experiences. This knowledge is a permanent preconscious grasp of the Infinite that forms the backdrop or horizon of our consciousness upon which we experience the finite.[1]

This inarticulable perception of God that silhouettes and adumbrates all of our experiences is the wellspring of desire out of which all of our seeking and choices arise. Robert Barron, commenting on the theology of Thomas Aquinas in this regard writes:

God is irresistibly present to the will as the ground of the will, precisely as the ultimate good that is always desired in any concrete act of the will. Whenever a person makes a particular choice—whether it is a trivial decision to see this movie rather than that or a significant decision to pursue a given career—she is, says Thomas, implicitly desiring her ultimate happiness. All individual acts of the will rest upon, depend upon, the final and all-embracing desire for the good itself—which is none other than God.[2]

Thus, God's all permeating presence to the soul by essence (substantial union), is the source of a permanent perception of God, be it ever so unconscious, that evokes a desire and longing for the Infinite.

So what does union by grace do? It makes us consciously aware of the utter intimacy that already exists between us and God as the result of substantial union. As Rahner puts it, it is "making explicit for ourselves what we already know implicitly about ourselves in the depths of our personal self-realization."[3] This is the rationale that underlies John's teaching on detachment; we detach ourselves of all that is not of God "so that God, who is naturally communicating himself to us through nature, may do so supernaturally through grace" (A 2. 5. 4).

The presence of God that is communicated through nature and through grace is not different in kind, but in intensity. This does not mean that God is *more* present to the soul through grace than through nature, but rather that the soul is more *conscious* of the utter intimacy of God that exists as a result of substantial union. This increase of consciousness happens because in the process of purification, the soul's capacity and receptivity for God has increased; it has made more "room for God" (A 2. 5. 7).

As John's metaphor of the painting implies (see below), grace increases our capacity to see the beauty that was *always present* before our eyes but which we hitherto only dimly perceived. This increase of sight we call faith (or contemplation), which is the conscious awareness of the soul's pre-reflective and preconscious knowledge of God.

This increase of the soul's knowledge of God is the result of grace alone, but it follows upon the soul's choice to love, which is the decision to "labor to divest and deprive oneself for God of all that is not God" (A 2. 5. 7).

Thus, for John, there is an interfacing and interaction between knowing and loving; they are inseparable. We can only love what we know, but only love has the power to disclose to us the true nature of what we love.

"the cleaner the window . . . the brighter will be its illumination" (A 2. 5. 6).

Finally, God's presence by spiritual affection, which the Bride in *The Spiritual Canticle* asks for, is a clear vision of the divine being and beauty but "since the conditions of this life will not allow such a manifestation, . . . God communicates to her some semi-clear glimpses of his divine beauty" (C 11. 3–4). Such glimpses are foretastes of eternal glory. Thus, there are not three *kinds* of presence that are disclosed to the soul, but three *degrees*: nature (preconscious awareness), grace (faith), and glory (beatific vision).

Metaphors of Union

The Window

To understand the nature of this union, one should first know that God sustains every soul and dwells in it substantially, even though it may be that of the greatest sinner in the world. This union between God and creatures always exists. By it he conserves their being so that if the union should end they would immediately be annihilated and cease to exist. . . . [W]e are not discussing [this type of union] that always exists, but the soul's union with and transformation in God that does not always exist, except where there is a likeness of love. We will call it the union of likeness; and the former, the essential or substantial union. . . . When the soul rids itself completely of what is repugnant and unconformed to the divine will, it rests transformed in God through love.

. . . And the soul will receive this likeness because nothing contrary to the will of God will be left in it. Thus, it will be transformed in God.

. . . Manifestly, then, the more that individuals through attachment and habit are clothed with their own abilities and with creatures, the less disposed they are for this union. For they do not afford God full opportunity to transform their souls into the supernatural. As a result, individuals have nothing more to do than strip their souls of these natural contraries and dissimilarities so that God, who is naturally communicating himself to them through nature, may do so supernaturally through grace.

. . . Here is an example that will provide a better understanding of this explanation. A ray of sunlight shining on a smudgy window is unable to illumine that window completely and transform it into its own light. It could do this if the window were cleaned and polished. The less the film and stain are wiped away, the less the window will be illuminated; and the cleaner the window is, the brighter will be its illumination. The extent of illumination is not dependent on the ray of sunlight but on the window. If the window is totally clean and pure, the sunlight will so transform and illumine it that to all appearances the window will be identical with the ray of sunlight and shine just as the sun's ray. Although obviously the nature of the window is distinct from that of the sun's ray . . . we can assert that the window is the ray or light of the sun by participation. The soul on which the divine light of God's being is ever shining, or better, in which it is ever dwelling by nature, is like this window. . . .

A soul makes room for God by wiping away all the smudges and smears of creatures, by uniting its will perfectly to God's; for to love is to labor to divest and deprive oneself for God of all that is not God. When this is done the soul will be illuminated by and transformed in God. And God will so communicate his supernatural being to the soul that it will appear to be God himself and will possess what God himself possesses (A 2. 5. 3–7).[4]

The Painting

The following example will also shed light on the nature of this union. Let us imagine a perfect painting with many finely wrought details and delicate, subtle adornments, including some so delicate and subtle that they are not wholly discernible. Now one whose sense of sight is not too clear and refined will discover less detail and delicacy in the painting; one whose vision is somewhat purer will discover more details and perfections; and another with yet clearer vision will find still more perfection; finally, the one who possesses the clearest faculty will discern the greatest number of excellent qualities and perfections. There is so much to behold in the painting that no matter how much one sees in it, still more remains unseen (A 2. 5. 9).

Fusion and Absorption

Just as in the consummation of carnal marriage there are two
in one flesh, . . . so also when the spiritual marriage between God
and the soul is consummated, there are two natures in one spirit
and love. . . . This union resembles the union of the light of a star
or candle with the light of the sun, for what then sheds light is
not the star or candle, but the sun, which has absorbed the other
lights into its own (C 22. 3).[5]

Notes

1. Karl Rahner, *Foundations of Christian Faith: An Introduction to the Idea of
Christianity,* trans. William V. Dych (New York: Crossroads Publishing Company, 1978), 51–65.

2. Robert Barron, *Thomas Aquinas: Spiritual Master* (New York: Crossroads
Publishing Coompny, 1996), 56.

3. Karl Rahner, *Foundations of Christian Faith,* 53.

4. Cf. F. 1, 13.

5. Mystics use different metaphors of one object being absorbed into another to try to explain the nature of union. Teresa of Avila writes in *The Interior Castle:* "Let us say that union [not full union but spiritual betrothal] is
like the joining of two wax candles to such an extent that the flame coming
from them is but one, or that the wick, the flame, and the wax are all one.
But afterward one candle can be easily separated from the other and there
are two candles; the same holds for the wick. In the spiritual marriage [on
the other hand] the union is like what we have when rain falls from the sky
into a river or fount; all is water, for the rain that fell from heaven cannot be
divided or separated from the water of the river. Or it is like what we have
when a little stream enters the sea, there is no means of separating the two.
Or, like the bright light entering a room through two different windows; although the streams of light are separate when entering the room, they become one" (7, 2, 4). "The Interior Castle," in *The Collected Works of St. Teresa of
Avila,* vol. 2., trans. Kieran Kavanaugh O.C.D. and Otilio Rodriguez (Washington, D.C.: ICS Publications, 1980), 434.

Desire, Desires, and Detachment

One common tenet shared by Christian theologians from Augustine to Aquinas and Dante down to John of the Cross and beyond is that since we are made in the image and likeness of God, our wills are so rooted in God as both our origin and destiny that in all of our choices we are seeking God either explicitly or implicitly as our final good. In short, we have no desire outside our root desire for God; all desires are sacramental and expressive of the one unifying desire of the human heart—the desire for God.

John expresses this truth by saying that all of our desires or appetites have both an *immediate* and *ultimate* object of satisfaction. For example, the immediate object of our appetite for food is to assuage the pangs of hunger that are expressive of our deepest hunger—hunger for God.

All of our appetites and their consequent pleasures and satiations are good, according to John, because God created them; nevertheless, they can become obstacles on the spiritual path if we become fixated or attached to them. John is not simply talking about our appetites for sensual pleasures, but anything that we choose to overinvest our ego in, be it our physical appearance, the acquisition of knowledge, or even the practice of virtue, to name a few.

Mortifying our inordinate desires does not lead to the elimination of desire, but rather the release of our deepest desire for God, which in turn, purifies, transforms, and integrates all of our other desires.

John compares our desire for God with the force of gravity. He says that if a rock (soul) were dropped to the surface of the earth, it would plummet to the earth's center (God) if it were not impeded by intervening objects. And just as the rock accelerates in speed the closer it comes to its center of gravity, so does a soul increase in desire for God the closer it comes to God. This image illustrates John's theology of detachment.

The Spanish word for detachment, *desprendimiento,* has a fundamentally positive thrust to it that is lost in translation; it does not merely refer to "giving up" something, but rather the laying down of something for the sake of something better.[1]

Detachment, mortification, self-denial, and any other negative sounding words that we encounter in John's writings need to be heard in the light of their overriding purpose—the attainment of our ultimate happiness in God.

In addition, a careful reading of John discloses that the mortification of our inordinate appetites expands the soul's capacity to "obtain more joy and recreation *in creatures* . . ." (A 3. 20. 2) and enables it to "reach out divinely to the enjoyment of all *earthly* and heavenly things, with a general freedom of spirit in them all" (N 2. 9. 1) (italic added).

The paradox of detachment that John sets before us is that only a non-possessive heart can truly possess and completely enjoy God's creation, for it is freed from the anxiety and fear that possessiveness engenders.

We have a symbol of this in Dickens' story *A Christmas Carol.* After Scrooge's transformation Dickens tells us:

> He went to church, and walked about the streets, and watched the people hurrying to and fro, and patted the children on the head, and questioned beggars, and looked down into the kitchens of houses, and up to the windows, and *found that everything could yield him pleasure*[2] (italic added).

Within the context of Dickens' story, I believe that he is saying that when we take a possessive, grasping, clutching stance toward life, as Scrooge did at the beginning of the story, we make ourselves miserable. It seems as if everything we try to possess balks and resists our entreaties. But when we approach creation with gentleness, reverence, respect, and non-possessive love, it *yields* to us what we are seeking: the pleasure, joy, and happiness that God intends for us to have.

This illustrates John's teaching, "To reach satisfaction in all desire satisfaction in nothing" (A 1. 13. 11). It is the paradox of the poor in spirit; they possess not only the earth but the heavens as well and can sing with John, "Mine are the heavens and mine are the earth . . ." (S 27), because they have come to discover a quality of joy that is not accessible to a possessive heart.

Possessiveness distorts our vision; we perceive life only from the

vantage point of self-interest—how things affect us. In contrast, a purified heart has the power and capacity to see things in all their radiant
beauty, truth, and native purity. In consequence, "Their joy . . . is far
different from the joy of one who is attached to [things for] . . . they
delight in these goods according to the truth of them, but those who are
attached delight according to what is false in them" (A 3. 20. 2).

John's teaching on desire is very complex but in broad strokes it may be
stated as follows: our *inordinate* desires are the source of all our suffering
and prevent us from seeing the world with unclouded eyes and
perceiving God's love for us; yet, John's teaching does not aim at the
elimination of our appetites but rather at their emancipation and transformation, so that our will and God's will become so completely one
that the soul "is no longer anything else than the appetite of God" (F 2.
34).

Freeing Our Desire for God

The deepest center of an object we take to signify the farthest point attainable by that object's being and power and force of operation and movement. So fire or a rock have the natural power and motion necessary to reach their center, but they cannot pass beyond it. They can fail to reach and rest in this center if a powerful contrary movement impedes them.

Accordingly, we assert that when a rock is in the ground it is, after a fashion, in its center, even though it is not in its deepest center, for it is within the sphere of its center, activity, and movement; yet we do not assert that it has reached its deepest center, which is the middle of the earth. Thus the rock always possesses the power, strength, and the inclination to go deeper and reach the ultimate and deepest center; and this it would do if the hindrance were removed. When once it arrives and no longer has any power or inclination toward further movement, we declare that it is in its deepest center.

The soul's center is God. When it has reached God with all the capacity of its being and the strength of its operation and inclination, it will have attained its final and deepest center in God, it will know, love and enjoy God with all its might. . . .

It is noteworthy, then, that love is the inclination, strength, and power for the soul making its way to God, for love unites it with God.[3] The more degrees of love it has, the more deeply it enters into God and centers itself in him. We can say that there are as many centers in God possible to the soul, each one deeper than the other, as there are degrees of love of God possible to it. A stronger love is a more unitive love, and we can understand in this manner the many mansions the Son of God declared were in his Father's house [Jn. 14:2].

Hence, for the soul to be in its center—which is God, as we have said—it is sufficient for it to possess one degree of love, for by one degree alone it is united with him through grace. Should it have two degrees, it becomes united and concentrated in God in another, deeper center. Should it reach three, it centers itself in a third. But once it has attained the final degree, God's love has arrived at wounding the soul in its ultimate and deepest center, which is to illuminate and transform it in its whole being, power, and strength, and according to its capacity, until it appears to be God (F 1. 11–13).

The Harm Done by Our Inordinate Desires[4]

The Privative Harm

To begin with, it is clear in speaking of the privative harm that a person by mere attachment to a created thing is less capable of God . . . (A 1. 6. 1).

For a . . . proof of this, it ought to be kept in mind that attachment to a creature makes a person equal to that creature; the stronger the attachment, the closer is the likeness to the creature and the greater the equality, for loves effects a likeness between the lover and the loved. . . .[5] By the mere fact that a soul loves something, it becomes incapable of pure union and transformation in God[6] (A 1. 4. 3–4).

The Positive Harms

Weariness

. . . [T]he [inordinate] appetites are wearisome and tiring.[7] They resemble little children, restless and hard to please, always whining to their mother for this thing or that and never satisfied (A. 1. 6. 5). This is the characteristic of those with appetites; they are always dissatisfied and bitter, like someone who is hungry (A 1. 6. 3).

Torment

Just as a peasant, covetous of the desired harvest, goads and torments the ox that pulls the plow, so concupiscence, in order to attain the object of its longing, afflicts the one who lives under the yoke of the appetites (A 1. 7. 1).[8]

Blindness

A moth is not helped much by its eyes because, blinded in its desire for the beauty of light, it will fly directly into a bonfire. . . . They [the appetites] enkindle concupiscence and overwhelm the intellect so that it cannot see its light. The reason is that a new light set directly in front of the visual faculty blinds this faculty so that it fails to see the light farther away (A 1. 8. 3).[9]

Defilement[10]

The fourth way the appetites harm the soul is by defiling and staining it. . . . [E]ach appetite leaves a deposit of filth and an unsightly mark in the soul (A 1. 9. 1, 4).

The gold, or the diamond, when placed on hot pitch becomes more stained and unsightly as the heat melting the pitch increases. Similarly, those who are fired by their appetite for some creature are stained and blackened by that creature because of the heat of their desire (A 1. 9. 1).

Weaken and lukewarm: The loss of our appetite for God

The appetites sap the strength needed for perseverance in the practice of virtue. Because the force of the desire is divided, the appetite becomes weaker than if it were completely fixed on one object. . . . A person whose will is divided among trifles is like water that leaking out at the bottom, will not rise higher and is therefore useless (A 1. 10. 1).[11]

The appetites . . . are like shoots burgeoning about a tree, sapping its strength, and causing it to be fruitless. . . . They are indeed like leeches always sucking blood from one's veins. . . .

How unhappy it [the soul] is with itself, how cold toward its neighbors, how sluggish and slothful in the things of God! No illness makes walking as burdensome, or eating as distasteful, as do the appetites for creatures render the practice of virtue burdensome and saddening to a person (A 1. 10. 2, 4).[12]

Recovering Our Appetite for God

If you desire that devotion be born in your spirit and that the love of God and the desire for divine things increase, cleanse your soul of every desire, attachment, and ambition in such a way that you have no concern about anything. Just as a sick person is immediately aware of good health once the bad humor has been thrown off and a desire to eat is felt, so will you recover your health, in God, if you cure yourself as was said (S 78).

Life-giving Detachment

Even if human beings do not free their heart of joy in temporal goods for the sake of God and the demands of Christian perfection, they ought to do so because of the resulting temporal advantages, prescinding from the spiritual ones. . . . [T]hey acquire the virtue of liberality. Liberality is one of God's principal attributes and can in no way coexist with covetousness.

Moreover, they acquire liberty of spirit, clarity of reason, rest, tranquility, peaceful confidence in God, and, in their will, the true cult and homage of God.

They obtain more joy and recreation in creatures through the dispossession of them. They cannot rejoice in them if they behold them with possessiveness, for this is a care that, like a trap, holds the spirit to earth and does not allow wideness of heart.

In detachment from things they acquire a clearer knowledge of them and a better understanding of both natural and supernatural truths concerning them. Their joy, consequently, in these temporal goods is far different from the joy of one who is attached to them, and they receive great benefits and advantages from their joy. They delight in these goods according to the truth in them, but those who are attached delight in the worst; they delight in the substance of them, those sensibly attached in the accidents.

Those, then, whose joy is unpossessive of things rejoice in them all as though they possessed them all; those others, beholding them with a possessive mind, lose all the delights of them in general. . . .

Cares do not molest the detached, neither in prayer nor outside it. . . . Yet those who are attached spend all their time going to and fro about the snare to which their heart is tied (A 3. 20. 2–3).

. . . [E]ven though this happy night darkens the spirit, it does so only to impart light concerning all things; and even though it humbles individuals and reveals their miseries, it does so only to exalt them; and even though it impoverishes and empties them of all possessions and natural affection, it does so only that they may reach out divinely to the enjoyment of all earthly and heavenly things, with a general freedom of spirit in them all (N 2. 9. 1).

If you purify your soul of attachments and desires, you will understand things spiritually. If you deny your appetites for them, you will enjoy their truth, understanding what is certain in them (S 49).

Consider that God reigns only in the peaceful and disinterested soul (S 71).

An Acquired Taste

That elements be commingled with all the natural compounds, they must be unaffected by any particular color, odor, or taste and thus they can concur with all tastes, odors, and colors. Similarly, the spirit must be simple, pure, and naked as to all natural affections, actual, and habitual in order to be able to communicate freely in fullness of spirit with the divine wisdom in which, on account of the soul's purity, the delights of all things are tasted to a certain eminent degree. Without this purgation the soul would be wholly unable to experience the satisfaction of all this abundance of spiritual delight. . . .

Because of their one attachment to the food and fleshmeat they had tasted in Egypt [cf. Ex. 16:3], the children of Israel were unable to get any taste from the delicate bread of angels—the manna in the desert (N 2. 9. 1–2).[13]

The Vast Dominion of the Non-possessive Heart

Mine are the heavens and mine is the earth. Mine are the nations, the just are mine, and mine the sinners. The angels are mine, and the Mother of God, and all things are mine; and God himself is mine and for me, because Christ is mine and all for me (S 27).[14]

Notes

1. For a fuller treatment of this see Glenys Edwards, *St. John of the Cross and Detachment* (Darlington, England: Darlington Carmel).

2. Charles Dickens, *A Christmas Carol and Other Christmas Stories* (New York: Penguin Books Ltd., 1984), 135.

3. The word translated in this passage as *love* in Spanish is *amor,* which can also be translated as desire. Throughout John's works love and desire are often used interchangeably.

4. There are two kinds of harm that our inordinate appetites cause the soul. The first and primary one is what John calls the *privative* harm, a state of being in which a soul is so absorbed in creatures that its capacity and receptivity to receive God's life are severely restricted; it becomes "less capable of God" (A 1. 6. 1). The second type of harm John calls the *positive* harms which are the emotional and psychological effects of our inordinate attachments; they blind, torment, darken, defile, and weaken us.

5. This is one of John's basic teachings, namely, that we tend to become like the thing we most consistently love.

6. Here is an example of John's "carelessness" in his writing. We can easily misinterpret this passage to mean that any desire or love that we have for a creature is an obstacle to our union with God. It is only in chapter eleven that John informs us that, "I am speaking of the voluntary appetites because the natural ones are of little or no hindrance at all to the attainment of union, provided they do not receive one's consent or pass beyond the first movements" (A 1. 11. 2). We need to keep in mind that the goal that John is focusing on is union of *wills.* It is our *choice* not our *inclinations* that leads us either toward God or away from God.

7. When John uses the word appetite, especially in the *Ascent,* it most frequently refers to our inordinate appetites.

8. The violence contained in this image underlines the compulsive nature of our inordinate appetites; they make us "driven." Compulsiveness is one of the qualities that modern psychologists use to differentiate normal

from pathological desire. See Karen Horney, *Neurosis and Human Growth* (New York: W. W. Norton & Co. 1950), esp. 29–31.

9. The blindness that John is talking about does not stem from *ignorance* of the danger that a situation involves, as the image of the moth and the flame suggests, but rather from an inordinate attachment to an object that makes the craving for that object so strong, that a soul will choose to pursue that object with an utter disregard for its own welfare.

10. The "first schema of evil" says Paul Ricoeur is defilement; it is primitive and harkens back to a time when the physical and moral universes were not clearly differentiated. One could become contaminated and rendered "unclean" merely by being exposed to certain objects. Because these primitive associations cling to the concept of defilement, it is often thought of as not worthy of our consideration. Yet, in spite of this, defilement as a category for sin contains a basic truth about human nature, namely, that every experience leaves its imprint upon us; every encounter deposits a residue recorded in memory. John's argument is basically this: if merely being exposed to or "touched" by something can affect us, *how much more* are we affected by something when we freely choose to reach out and "touch" it with the desire of the will.

11. The term "the appetite" in this passage refers to the will.

12. This author does not believe that it is by accident that John mentions weakness and tepidity last, for they are symptomatic of the death of desire. In the light of what has already been said about the centrality of desire as the soul's impetus in spiritual life, lack of desire is the most harmful of all conditions. The images that John uses to describe this state (sapping of strength, sucking of blood, sluggishness, slothfulness, etc.) speak of a spiritual depression that renders desire anemic. John's images are descriptive of acedia (sloth) the state of soul that Saint John Climacus calls the deadliest of all sins, for where there is no desire, there is no life.

13. C. S. Lewis once said that in our present state, the joys of heaven are an "acquired taste." John says the same regarding true joy in this present life. He uses the metaphor of manna several times in his writings to express the necessity of cleansing our palate of inordinate desires in order to "taste" true joy. Cf. A 1. 5. 3, 5. 8; N 1. 9. 4, 2. 9. 2; F 3. 38. In the state of union our "palate is all bathed in glory and love" (F 1. 1).

14. This prayer reflects the teaching of Saint Thérèse regarding the blessings that flow from not being either possessive or envious of another's gifts. Thérèse paraphrasing Tauler once said, "If I love the good that is in my neighbor as much as he loves it in himself, that good is as much mine as it is his. Through this communion I can enrich myself with all the good there is in heaven and on earth, in the angels, in the saints and in all those who love God." Christopher O'Mahony, ed. and trans., *St. Thérèse of Lisieux: By Those who Knew Her* (Dublin: Veritas Publications, 1975), 125.

Entering the Dark Night

Chapter thirteen of the first book of the *Ascent* is one of the most well-known and frequently quoted sections of John's writings; it contains "counsels and methods" on how to actively enter the dark night. John calls these instructions "an abridged method" of entering the dark night.

The abridged nature of these counsels is beneficial in that it helps us to focus on essential disciplines for the spiritual journey, but it also makes them potentially dangerous; for anything abbreviated in the spiritual life becomes susceptible to misinterpretation.

The terseness of these counsels in combination with their stark style and a lack of examples that would clarify their meaning renders them difficult to interpret. In consequence, the reader should constantly be asking the text: "What do these counsels really mean when I translate them into my daily life?"

The Imitation of Christ

First, have habitual desire to imitate Christ in all your deeds by bringing your life into conformity with his. You must then study his life in order to know how to imitate him and behave in all events as he would[1] (A 1. 13. 3).

Remaining Empty

Second, in order to be successful in this imitation, renounce and remain empty of any sensory satisfaction that is not purely for the honor and glory of God. Do this out of love for Jesus Christ. In his life he had no other gratification, nor desired any other, than the fulfillment of his Father's will, which he called his meat and food [Jn. 4:34].[2]

For example, if you are offered the satisfaction of hearing things that have no relation to the service and glory of God, do not desire this pleasure or the hearing of these things. When you have an opportunity for the gratification of looking upon objects that will not help you love God more, do not desire this gratification or sight. And if in speaking there is a similar opportunity, act in the same way. And so on with all the senses insofar as you can duly avoid such satisfaction. If you cannot escape the experience of this satisfaction, it will be sufficient to have no desire for it[3] (A 1. 13. 3–4).

The Blessings of Mortification

By this method you should endeavor, then, to leave the senses as through in darkness, mortified and empty of that satisfaction. With such vigilance you will gain a great deal in a short time.

Many blessings flow when the four natural passions (joy, hope, fear, and sorrow) are in harmony and at peace. The following maxims contain a complete method for mortifying and pacifying them. If put into practice these maxims will give rise to abundant merit and great virtues.[4]

Endeavor to be inclined always:[5]

> not to the easiest, but to the most difficult;
> not to the most delightful, but to the most distasteful;
> not to the most gratifying, but to the less pleasant;
> not to what means rest for you, but to hard work;
> not to the consoling, but to the unconsoling;
> not to the most, but to the least;
> not to the highest and most precious, but to the lowest and the most despised;
> not to wanting something, but to wanting nothing.

Do not go about looking for the best of temporal things, but for the worst, and, for Christ, desire to enter into complete nakedness, emptiness, and poverty in everything in the world.

You should embrace these practices earnestly and try to overcome the repugnance of your will toward them. If you sincerely put them into practice with order and discretion, you will discover in them great delight and consolation[6] (A 1. 13. 4–7).

Holy Contempt

[H]ere is another exercise that teaches mortification of concupiscence of the flesh, concupiscence of the eyes, and pride of life, which, as Saint John says, reign in the world and give rise to all the other appetites [1 Jn. 2:16].

First, try to act with contempt for yourself and desire that all others do likewise. Second, endeavor to speak in contempt of yourself and desire all others to do so. Third, try to think lowly and contemptuously of yourself and desire that all others do the same[7] (A 1. 13. 8–9).

Counsels for Climbing Mount Carmel[8]

To reach satisfaction in all
   desire satisfaction in nothing.
To come to possess all
   desire the possession of nothing.
To arrive at being all
   desire to be nothing.
To come to the knowledge of all
   desire the knowledge of nothing.

To come to enjoy what you have not
   you must go by a way in which you enjoy not.
To come to the knowledge you have not
   you must go by a way in which you know not.
To come to the possession you have not
   you must go by a way in which you possess not.
To come to be what you are not
   you must go by a way in which you are not[9]
(A 1. 13. 11).

Alacrity of Response

When you delay in something
you cease to rush toward the all.
For to go from the all to the all
you must deny yourself of all in all.
And when you come to the possession of the all
you must possess it without wanting anything.
Because if you desire to have something in all
your treasure in God is not purely your all[10]
(A 1. 13. 12).

Conclusion

In this nakedness the spirit finds its quietude and rest. For in coveting nothing, nothing tires it by pulling it up and nothing oppresses it by pushing it down, because it is in the center of its humility. When it covets something, by this very fact it tires itself (A 1. 13. 13).

Notes

1. A cursory reading of this counsel seems to indicate that it is nothing more than an admonition to meditate on the Scriptures (the Spanish word that is translated study is *considerar,* which means to "to consider," "to ponder," "to reflect upon"). But on closer examination, this council reveals part of John's psychology of desire, namely, that desire is sustained by the choices we make ". . . have habitual desire (*ordinario apetito*) . . . *by* bringing your life into conformity with his" (italic added).

2. John is not advocating some impersonal Stoicism but rather an asceticism that is a loving response to the person of Jesus Christ. "Do this out of love (*amor*) for Jesus Christ."

3. These admonitions to deny one's appetites on the sensual level must be understood as a *means* of awakening our desire for God, for the less our consciousness is absorbed in the desire for sensual gratification, the more we are awakened to the presence of God. Perhaps the best commentary on this passage of John's is Hopkins's poem *The Habit of Perfection* in which the poet writes of mortifying the senses as a means of accessing the spiritual dimension of life. "Be shelled, eyes, with double dark/And find the uncreated light:/This ruck and reel which you remark/Coils, keeps, and teases simple sight."

4. The Greeks and mediaeval scholastics connected the virtue of temperance with beauty and aesthetics for it brings order, harmony, and symmetry into our lives. Josep Pieper writes: "The purpose and goal of *temperantia* is man's inner order, from which alone 'serenity of spirit' can flow forth." Richard and Clara Winston, trans., *The Four Cardinal Virtues* (New York: Harcourt, Brace & World, Inc., 1965), 145. John often underlines the harmony and peace that ensue from mortification. Cf.A 1. 13. 13; 3. 20. 2–3.

5. It is important to note that John does not say to *do* the most difficult thing, etc., but rather to *be inclined* to do the most difficult thing, etc. He is speaking about a readiness, an openness, an attentive state of mind that

stands in vigilance to do God's will. This mental stance, which is a sustained act of the will, makes a person conscious of the presence of God because it alters a person's consciousness.

6. There are basically two ways that we can begin to understand the "delight and consolation" derived from practicing the mortification of the appetites that John proposes. The first is by considering the state of a person's life whose will is always inclined toward the easiest, the most delightful, etc. If we do so, I think we will discover that a way of being which is characterized by always seeking the easy way out of things, taking the path of least resistance, or doing the minimum, etc., is a formula for misery. Whenever the inclination of our will is *seeking* some form of pleasure or trying to avoid some form of discomfort, by contrast, everything becomes a burden; the least amount of effort saps one's strength; any request is experienced as an imposition, and every difficulty or discomfort is exaggerated. Why? Because life is constantly frustrating desire.

Secondly, just as Jesus found his "meat and food" in doing his Father's will (A 1. 13. 4), we too are nourished on a deep spiritual level when we live out of a habitual desire to do God's will. We experience this nourishment because when we are inclined to do God's will, we are united to both our deepest will and God's will that connects us to our true selves.

7. These counsels are very difficult to understand and are highly susceptible to misinterpretation. They seem to be advocating a type of masochistic self-hate, but there is no evidence either in the writings or life of John to substantiate such a viewpoint. The reader must interpret them through the lens of the purpose of the counsels, which is to aid us in mortifying our *inordinate appetites*. Thus, the "contempt" that John is referring to is not to be directed to us as beautiful creatures made in God's image and likeness, but rather to our egotistical patterns of thinking, speaking, and acting that prevent us from growing in God's love. Thus, the core of these counsels is to choose not to act upon our inner tendency toward self idolatry that manifests itself in our thoughts, words, and actions. For a good explanation of these counsels see Norbert Cummins O.C.D., *Freedom to Rejoice: Understanding St. John of the Cross* (London: Harper Collins Pub. Co., 1991), 88–9.

8. These counsels are contained on John's drawing entitled "The Mount of Perfection" or "Mount Carmel."

9. Again, John is underlining the importance of non-possessiveness and is also speaking about a fundamental truth of life, namely, that we can never obtain happiness by seeking it *directly* because happiness only *follows upon* doing God's will. This is a basic principle of John's spirituality (Cf. A 3. 17. 2). Viktor Frankl expressed this truth in more secular terms by the following: "I admonish my students . . . 'Don't aim at success; the more you aim at it and make it a target the more you are going to miss it. For success, like happiness, cannot be pursued; it must ensue and it only does so as the unintended side-effect of one's personal dedication to a cause greater than oneself or as the by-product of one's surrender to a person other than one-

self.'" Viktor E. Frankl, *Man's Search for Meaning,* trans. Ilse Lasch (New York: Simon & Schuster, 1984), 12.

10. The two words that John seems to be contrasting here are delay (*reparas*) and rush (*arrojarte*). *Reparas* has the connotation of delay in order to consider or reflect upon; whereas, *arrojarte* can be translated metaphorically as embarking upon an enterprise with a certain abandon. Thus, John may be cautioning us about the danger of being overly circumspect, lest we give fear, selfishness, etc., enough space to talk us out of doing God's will.

Positively, John is speaking about practicing an alacrity in our response that is a characteristic of the love of a soul in union (C 28. 5). This promptness of response is also one of the chief qualities of love that Saint Francis de Sales says is characteristic of perfect love. See *Introduction to the Devout Life,* Part 1, chapter 1.

The Imperfections of Beginners

God aids "beginners" in their attempts at changing their lives by showering them with sensible consolations for the sake of weaning them away from the things of this world. However, for many souls, these consolations prove to be more of a hindrance than a help on the spiritual path; they "let themselves be encumbered by the very consolations and favors God bestows on them for the sake of their advancing" (A Prol.7). In chapters two through seven of book one of the *Dark Night,* using the seven capital sins as his framework, John gives a penetrating analysis of the various ways that the experience of consolation encumbers these souls, but as varied as these ways are, they all stem from two sources, egocentricity and addiction to pleasure.

Egocentricity

Consolation does not *cause* the various manifestations of egocentricity that John describes but rather provides experiences that can easily be interpreted from a narcissistic point of view. "Because God is giving me these experiences, I must be special." However, such experiences do not automatically produce such an ego-inflating interpretation, for John tells us that some souls receive God's consolation with humility. John seems to indicate that what determines the effect that consolation has upon a person is his or her degree of narcissism. With great psychological acumen, John describes the predominant traits of a narcissistic personality disorder that are frequently manifested in "beginners": a grandiose sense of self-importance, intolerance to criticism, exhibitionism, the need to be the center of attention, and feeling threatened

73

when someone else vies for the limelight. John says that all these manifestations of egocentricity are purified in the dark night.

Addiction to Pleasure

Like children, "beginners" are ruled by the pleasure principle; they seek
to obtain sensual satisfaction and avoid discomfort and try to manufac-
ture feelings by overindulging themselves in spiritual exercises, and,
conversely, they avoid any spiritual discipline that is distasteful. They
are easily bored and become angry and peevish when their attempts to
obtain satisfaction are frustrated. "And if they do not get what they
want, they become sad and go away like testy children" (N 1. 6. 3).
Children is one of the metaphors that John uses most frequently to
describe "beginners" addicted to the pleasure of consolation (cf. A Prol.
3; 2. 14. 3; 2. 17. 6; 2. 17. 7; 2. 19. 6; 2. 21. 3; 3. 28. 7; 3. 39. 1; N 1. 1. 2; 1. 1.
3; 1. 3. 1; 1. 5. 1; 1. 6. 3; 1. 6. 6; 1. 12. 1).

Pride

These beginners feel so fervent and diligent in their spiritual exercises and undertakings that a certain kind of secret pride is generated in them that begets a complacency with themselves and their accomplishments. . . . Then they develop a somewhat vain . . . desire to speak of spiritual things in others' presence, and sometimes even to instruct rather than be instructed; in their hearts they condemn others who do not seem to have the kind of devotion they would like them to have, and sometimes they give expression to this criticism . . .

Some of these persons become so evil-minded that they do not want anyone except themselves to appear holy; and so by both word and deed they condemn and detract others whenever the occasion arises. . . .

And when at times their spiritual directors, their confessors, or their superiors disapprove their spirit and method of procedure, they feel that these directors do not understand, or perhaps that this failure to approve derives from a lack of holiness, since they want these directors to regard their conduct with esteem and praise. So they quickly search for some other spiritual adviser more to their liking, someone who will congratulate them and be impressed by their deeds. . . . Sometimes they want others to recognize their spirit and devotion, and as a result occasionally contrive ceremonies . . . for others to take notice of these.

Many want to be the favorites of their confessors, and thus they are consumed by a thousand envies and disquietudes. Embarrassment forbids them from relating their sins clearly, lest their reputation diminish in their confessor's eyes. They confess their sins in the most favorable light so as to appear better than they actually are . . . [and] they confess the evil things they do to a different confessor. . . .

Sometimes they minimize their faults, and at other times they become discouraged by them, since they felt they were already saints, and they become impatient and angry with themselves. . . .

They are often extremely anxious that God remove their faults and imperfections, but their motive is personal peace rather than God. They fail to realize that were God to remove their faults they might well become more proud and presumptuous (N 1. 2. 1–5).

Avarice

Many beginners also at times possess great spiritual avarice. They hardly ever seem content with the spirit God gives them. They become unhappy and peevish because they don't find the consolation they want in spiritual things. Many never have enough of hearing counsels, or learning spiritual maxims, or keeping them and reading books about them.[1]

Furthermore, they weigh themselves down with over-decorated images and rosaries. They now put these down, now take up others; at one moment they are exchanging, and at the next reexchanging.

What I condemn in this is possessiveness of heart and attachment to the number, workmanship, and over-decoration of these objects (N 1. 3. 1).

Lust

[S]piritual persons have numerous imperfections, many of which can be called spiritual lust, not because the lust is spiritual but because it proceeds from spiritual things. It happens frequently that in a person's spiritual exercises themselves, without the person being able to avoid it, impure movements will be experienced in the sensory part of the soul, and even sometimes when the spirit is deep in prayer or when receiving the sacraments of Penance or the Eucharist. These impure feelings arise from any of three causes outside of one's control.

First, they often proceed from the pleasure human nature finds in spiritual exercises. Since both the spiritual and the sensory part of the soul receive gratification from that refreshment, each part experiences delight according to its own nature and properties.[2]

The second origin of these rebellions is the devil. . . . [He] excites these feelings while souls are at prayer, instead of when they are engaged in other works, so that they might abandon prayer.

The third origin from which these impure feelings usually proceed and wage war on the soul is the latter's fear of them.[3] The fear that springs up at the sudden remembrance of these thoughts, caused by what one sees, is dealing with, or thinking of, produces impure feelings without the person being at fault (N 1. 4. 1–4).

Anger

Because of the strong desire of many beginners for spiritual gratification, they usually have many imperfections of anger. When the delight and satisfaction procured in their spiritual exercises passes . . . they become peevish in the works they do and easily angered by the least thing . . . just as a child is when withdrawn from the sweet breast.

Among these spiritual persons there are also those who fall into another kind of spiritual anger. Through a certain indiscreet zeal they become angry over the sins of others, reprove these others, and sometimes even feel the impulse to do so angrily, which in fact they occasionally do, setting themselves up as lords of virtue.

Others, in becoming aware of their own imperfections, grow angry with themselves in an unhumble impatience (N 1. 5. 1–3).

Gluttony

These imperfections [of spiritual gluttony] arise because of the delight beginners find in their spiritual exercises.

Many, lured by the delight and satisfaction procured in their religious practices, strive more for spiritual savor than for spiritual purity and discretion, . . . Some, attracted by the delight they feel in their spiritual exercises, kill themselves with penances, and others weaken themselves by fasts. . . .

And like beasts, they are motivated in these penances by an appetite for the pleasure they find in them.

In receiving Communion they spend their time trying to get some feeling and satisfaction rather than humbly praising and reverencing God dwelling within them. And they go about this in such a way that, if they do not procure any sensible feeling and satisfaction, they think they have accomplished nothing.

They have the same defect in their prayer, for they think the whole matter consists in looking for sensory satisfaction and devotion. They strive to procure this by their own efforts, and tire and weary their heads and their faculties. When they do not get this sensible comfort, they become very disconsolate and think they have done nothing. . . . Once they do not find delight in prayer, or in any other spiritual exercise, they feel extreme reluctance and repugnance in returning to it and sometimes even give it up. . . . [For] they are like children who are prompted to act not by reason but by pleasure (N 1. 6. 1–6).

Those who are always attached to them [sensible things], and never become detached, will never stop being like a little child, or speaking of God as a child, or knowing and thinking of God as a child (A 2. 17. 6).

This is why it is important for these beginners to enter the dark night and be purged of this childishness (N 1. 6. 6).

Envy and Sloth

In regard to envy, many of them feel sad about the spiritual good of others and experience sensible grief in noting that their neighbor is ahead of them on the road of perfection, and they do not want to hear others praised. Learning of the virtues of others makes them sad. They cannot bear to hear others being praised without contradicting and undoing these compliments as much as possible.

Also, regarding spiritual sloth, these beginners usually become weary in exercises that are more spiritual and flee from them since these exercises are contrary to sensory satisfaction. Since they are so used to finding delight in spiritual practices, they become bored when they do not find it.

Many of these beginners want God to desire what they want, and they become sad if they have to desire God's will. They feel an aversion toward adapting their will to God's. Hence they frequently believe that what is not their will, or brings them no satisfaction, is not God's will, and, on the other hand, that if they are satisfied, God is too. They measure God by themselves and not themselves by God (N 1. 7. 1–3).[4]

Notes

1. This is a manifestation of what John says is the chief characteristic of those who have appetites. "They are always dissatisfied and bitter" (A 1. 6. 3).

2. This is an example of John's view that human nature is a unified whole of "sense" and "spirit" (cf. N 2. 1. 1; 3. 1; F 1. 10).

3. John does not offer any reason why the *fear* of impure thoughts actually produces them, but I believe that there are at least two possible reasons why this is the case. First, aversion is a form of attention; trying *not* to think of something is a way of attending to it; we give power to the things that we resist. Second, the physiological manifestations of fear are very similar to those of sexual arousal (e.g., one's heartbeat and breathing increases; one begins to perspire, etc.) In consequence, just as any sensation has the tendency to trigger memories that are associated with that sensation (e.g., smelling a particular perfume will trigger memories of a person who is associated with the scent of that perfume), so will the sensations associated with sexual arousal trigger memories of being sexually aroused.

4. See F 4. 8 for examples of how we project upon both God and our neighbor. "Such is the lowliness of our condition in this life; for we think others are like ourselves and we judge others according to what we ourselves are" (F 4. 8).

The Beginnings of Contemplation

God usually showers a soul with consolations "after it has been reso-lutely converted to his service" (N 1. 1. 1) in order to draw the "beginner" away from an old way of life. However, in due time, these consolations cease, then the "passive night of the senses" begins.

What is the nature of this night? "This night . . . is contemplation" (N 1. 8. 1), which is "God's self-communication" (A 2. 15. 2), a mode of God's presence that John describes as "serene limpid light" (A 2. 15. 3), a "general loving knowledge of God" (A 2. 13. 7) that is experienced as a "loving or peaceful awareness" (A 2. 15. 2).

However, since the "beginner" is accustomed to and usually attached to experiencing God as palpable consolation, he or she will often fail to notice the delicate and subtle way that God is present in contemplation. For unlike consolation, contemplation, especially when it is first being communicated to the soul, is "extremely subtle and delicate, almost imperceptible." Consequently, the soul "hardly perceives or feels this new insensible, purely spiritual experience" (A 2. 13. 7). Thus, because God is no longer present as consolation, and the soul is unable to perceive God as contemplation, it believes that God is absent; every-thing feels "dry and empty" (N 1. 9. 4). So how does the soul know whether this dryness is the result of the dark night or some other cause such as laxity or illness?

John gives three signs to help the soul discern this question; he gives them in both the *Dark Night* and the *Ascent.* His treatment of the signs in both works is very similar, but there is one important difference. In the *Ascent,* John underlines the soul's desire "to remain alone in loving awareness of God without particular considerations, in interior peace and quiet and repose . . ." (A 2. 13. 4). This sense of being at home with the simple awareness of God's presence is not found in John's version of

79

the three signs in the *Dark Night*. One of the common explanations for this difference is that in the *Ascent,* John describes a soul that has become accustomed to contemplation; whereas, in the *Dark Night* John describes a person in whom this simple awareness of God's presence is new.

The reader must also keep in mind that even though John focuses on the experience of dryness during times of prayer, the "passive night of the senses" extends to the whole of life; practicing the virtues becomes difficult, religious exercises become tedious, etc.

The Three Signs

The Dark Night

The first [sign] is that since these souls do not get satisfaction or consolation from the things of God, they do not get any from creatures either. . . . Through this sign it can in all likelihood be inferred that this dryness and distaste is not the outcome of newly committed sins and imperfections. If this were so, some inclination or propensity to look for satisfaction in something other than the things of God would be felt in the sensory part, for when the appetite is allowed indulgence in some imperfection, the soul immediately feels an inclination toward it. . . .

Yet, because the want of satisfaction in earthly or heavenly things could be the product of some indisposition or melancholic humor, which frequently prevents one from being satisfied with anything, the second sign or condition is necessary.[1]

The second sign for the discernment of this purgation is that the memory ordinarily turns to God solicitously and with painful care, and thinks it is not serving God but turning back, because it is aware of this distaste for the things of God. Hence it is obvious that this aversion and dryness is not the fruit of laxity and tepidity, for lukewarm people do not care much for the things of God nor are they inwardly solicitous about them.

There is, consequently, a notable difference between dryness and lukewarmness. The lukewarm are very lax and remiss in their will and spirit, and have no solicitude about serving God. Those suffering from the purgative dryness are ordinarily solicitous, concerned, and pained about not serving God. Even though the dryness may be furthered by melancholia or some other humor—as it often is—it does not thereby fail to produce its purgative effect in the appetite. . . . If this humor is the entire cause, everything ends in displeasure and does harm to one's nature, and there are none of these desires to serve God that accompany the purgative dryness. . . .[2] The third sign . . . is the powerlessness, in spite of one's efforts, to meditate and make use of the imagination . . . as was one's previous custom (N 1. 9. 2–3. 8).

The Ascent

The first [sign] is the realization that one cannot make discursive meditation or receive satisfaction from it as before.[3] Dryness is now the outcome of fixing the senses on subjects that formerly provided satisfaction. However, as long as one can make discursive meditation and draw out satisfaction, one must not abandon this method. Meditation must be discontinued only when the soul is placed in that peace and quietude to be spoken of in the third sign.

The second sign is an awareness of a disinclination to fix the imagination or sense faculties on other particular objects, exterior or interior. I am not affirming that the imagination will cease to come and go—even in deep recollection it usually wanders freely—but that the person does not want to fix it purposely on extraneous things.

The third and surest sign is that a person likes to remain alone in loving awareness of God, without particular considerations, in interior peace and quiet and repose, and without the acts and exercises (at least discursive, those in which one progresses from point to point) of the intellect, memory and will. Such a one prefers to remain only in the general loving awareness and knowledge . . . without any particular knowledge or understanding. To leave safely the state of meditation and sense and enter that of contemplation and spirit, spiritual persons must observe within themselves at least these three signs together[4] (A 2. 13. 2–5).

The Cause of the Dark Night of the Senses

The reason for this dryness is that God transfers his goods and strength from sense to spirit. Since the sensory part of the soul is incapable of the goods of spirit, it remains deprived, dry and empty. Thus, while the spirit is tasting, the flesh tastes nothing at all and becomes weak in its work (N 1. 9. 4).

The Soul Does Not Experience God's Presence

If in the beginning the soul does not experience this spiritual savor and delight, but dryness and distaste, the reason is the novelty involved in this exchange. Since its palate is accustomed to these sensory tastes, the soul still sets its eyes on them. And since, also, its spiritual palate is neither purged nor accommodated for so subtle a taste, it is unable to experience the spiritual savor and good until gradually prepared by means of this dark and obscure night. The soul instead experiences dryness and distaste because of a lack of the gratification it formerly enjoyed so readily (N 1. 9. 4).

This is especially so when through failure to understand it [the loving knowledge that is being communicated to the soul] one does not permit oneself to rest in it but strives after the other more sensory experience. Although the interior peace is more abundant, the individual allows no room to experience and enjoy it (A 2. 13. 7). [It] has not made within itself a peaceful place for it (N 1. 11. 1).

But the more habituated persons become to this calm, the more their experience of this general loving knowledge of God will increase. This knowledge is more enjoyable than all other things because without the soul's labor it affords peace, rest, savor, and delight (A 2. 13. 7).

How the Soul Should Conduct Itself in this Dark Night

The attitude necessary in the night of sense is to pay no attention to discursive meditation since this is not the time for it. They should allow the soul to remain in rest and quietude even though it may seem obvious to them that they are doing nothing and wasting time, and even though they think this disinclination to think about anything is due to their laxity. Through patience and perseverance in prayer, they will be doing a great deal without activity on their part.

All that is required of them here is freedom of soul, that they liberate themselves from the impediment and fatigue of ideas and thoughts, and care not about thinking and meditating. They must be content simply with a loving and peaceful attentiveness to God, and live without the concern, without the effort, and without the desire to taste or feel him. All these desires disquiet the soul and distract it from the peaceful, quiet, and sweet idleness of the contemplation that is being communicated to it (N 1. 10. 4–5).

[These souls] should learn to remain in God's presence with a loving attention and a tranquil intellect, even though they seem to be idle. For little by little and very soon the divine calm and peace with a wondrous, sublime knowledge of God, enveloped in divine love, will be infused into their souls (A 2. 15. 5).

What we need most in order to make progress is to be silent before this great God with our appetite and with our tongue, for the language he best knows is silent love (S 132).

Notes

1. One of the most common symptoms of depression (melancholia) is anhedonia, which is a pervasive loss of interest or ability to experience pleasure in activities that a person normally finds enjoyable.

2. Even though John differentiates depression (melancholia) from the dark night, he says that a certain amount of depression will often accom-

pany the dark night as one of its effects. The reason why this happens is that when the soul is experiencing the dark night, it feels that it has "lost" God. Loss is one one of the common causes of depression.

3. What John means by discursive meditation is a method of prayer by which the mind uses the interior faculties of the intellect, memory, and will in a step by step procedure to ponder some spiritual subject (usually a scene from the Gospels) for the sake of evoking acts of praise, love, thanksgiving, etc. One of the best-known methods of discursive meditation in John's day was that set down by Saint Ignatius of Loyola in his *Spiritual Exercises*.

4. As a person grows in prayer, there is a natural tendency for prayer to become less discursive and more simplified. Contemplation, as John uses the word, does not refer to either this process of simplification or the effects of peace and calm that ensue from using a particular technique (e.g., mantra). Contemplation is the direct result of grace alone. In consequence, John is cautioning his readers not to abandon discursive meditation in order to achieve a "higher state" of prayer. Saint Teresa gives the same advice. (Cf. *The Book of Her Life,* chapter 12. 5; *The Interior Castle,* 4. 3. 7).

The Active Night of the Spirit: Faith

In books two and three of the *Ascent,* John deals with the purification and transformation of the three faculties of intellect, memory, and will by means of the theological virtues of faith, hope, and love respectively. John's treatment of this central part of the spiritual life will often sound very impersonal and mechanical because the language of scholastic theology that he employs has a tendency to reify both our psychological functions and the virtues. However, in John's writings, the theological virtues, "especially faith, are so deeply tied in with contemplative prayer that they might even appear to become synonymous with it."[1] Therefore, as the reader approaches the text, he or she must keep several things in mind. First, the theological virtues transform the human person into God by participation because the virtues are not "things" but the impact that God's presence (contemplation) has on the different capacities or faculties of the soul. For example, as the light of God's grace illuminates the soul's powers of perception, thinking, and knowing (intellect) it grows in knowledge of God, for faith "communicates God himself . . ." and "terminates through the clear vision of God" (C 12. 4). Even in this life, the light of faith so transforms the soul's vision that it begins to see through the eyes of God so to speak. Thus, John says of the soul in union: "The soul knows creatures through God and not God through creatures" (F 4. 5).

However, the light that faith gives is paradoxical for it is often experienced as darkness, especially when it shines in the soul with all its brilliance; for like the light of the Sun that causes blindness because it overwhelms the eye's capacity to receive its intensity, so does the light of faith exceed the intellect's capacity to grasp what is being communicated to it. (A 2. 3. 1)

Another reason why the light of faith is often not grasped by the soul to whom it is communicated is the *nature* of the knowledge that is being imparted. The intellect is accustomed to knowledge as it is received through the five senses, in the form of clear distinct bits of information. In contrast, the knowledge that faith confers bypasses the senses and is received directly through the spirit, not in the form of clear and distinct concepts and ideas but as a "vague, dark, and general knowledge" (A 2. 10. 4). This general knowledge is apprehended on the level of intuition and instinct. Saint Thérèse spoke of being guided by the light of faith as a "felt sense." "He teaches without noise of words. Never have I heard him speak, but I feel that he is within me, at each moment; he is guiding and inspiring me with what to say and do."[2]

This "felt sense" is a mode of knowing that John says "brings certitude" but "does not produce clarity" (A 2. 6. 2). We may compare the experience of this type of knowing to peripheral vision. As I sit here at my desk I am *certain* that I see the lamp that is on my left side, but my vision of it is not focused; it is *not clear*.

The presence of God in our lives is something like my lamp; it is always there, and I am always *perceiving* it out of the corner of my eye, but I am not always *consciously aware* of it because I'm not always *attending to* it. Attending to the quiet simple presence of God in the soul as contemplation is the primal act of faith for John. As Ross Collings puts it, "This steady commitment of attentiveness into the dark region where God is spiritually 'sensed' is what John means by 'acquiring' contemplative faith."[3] It is only within this perspective that we can understand the nature of the asceticism that John is advocating in books two and three of the *Ascent*. The reason the soul must "depart from all natural phantasms and intellectual reasonings . . ." (A 2. 1. 2) is that "we are imparting instructions . . . for advancing in contemplation" (A 3. 2. 2).

To understand what John is saying here, the reader must keep in mind the specific audience that he is writing to; books two and three of the *Ascent* are addressed to souls that have discerned that God is imparting the loving knowledge of his presence (contemplation) to them. Books two and three of the *Ascent* deal with "the active night of the spirit" which is the soul's *response* to the inflow of God (passive night of the senses). Thus, the main asceticism that is required of the soul is to listen. This requires that the soul do two things: first, to quiet the mind and be careful not to allow consciousness to become entangled and absorbed in the noise of thoughts during times of prayer, and, second, to continue to divest the soul of inordinate appetites and attachments that keep the soul ignorant of God's wisdom. "If you purify your soul of attachments and desires, you will understand things spiritually" (S 49). The goal of both exercises is to allow the voice of God (faith) to be one's guide. "By blinding one's faculties along this road, one will see light. . . . Those who both live in darkness and blind themselves to all natural lights will have supernatural vision, and those who want to lean on some light of their own will become blind and be held back on this road leading to union" (A 2. 4. 7).

Is John saying that we should not listen to the voices of reason, common sense, and the counsel from others? By no means. All of these things have their place in the spiritual life. However, the light of faith is a brighter light than that of reason, and like the sun "will eclipse and suppress a dimmer one" (A 2. 3. 1). John is saying that while we should not disdain the light of reason, when we are "*attached* to any understanding, feeling, imagining, opinion, desire, or way of our own . . ." (A 2. 4. 4) (italic added), the soul will not be completely open to be led by that "felt sense," the light that contemplation imparts.

In consequence, John says that we must "blind" ourselves to these lesser lights so we can grow in our perception and trust of God's Light (A 2. 4. 3). In H. G. Wells' novel, *The Invisible Man,* the protagonist feared the blind because since they were not able to rely upon their sight, they developed "subtle intuitions" that allowed them to see what was invisible. The same is true with faith; it is a "blindness" that allows the soul to "see" the invisible God. "The more darkness it [faith] brings on them, the more light it sheds. For by blinding, it illuminates them. . . ." (A 2. 3. 4).

As our faith becomes more illuminated by the subtle general knowledge of God's presence, we should not think that the God revealed in Jesus Christ and the articles of the Creed gives way to a belief in some amorphous, unthematic, divine force. When John compares the articles of faith to the outer expression ("silvered-over faces") of the underlying substance that they manifest ("gold") (C 12. 4) he is not saying that they are different from one another, but rather that our *understanding* of what has been revealed in the Creed is "like a sketch" (C 12. 1) that will be fully disclosed to us in the Beatific Vision. For John, Christ is the ultimate object of faith that discloses to us the fulness of God (A 2. 22. 5–6). This is the divinity that is revealed in the general knowledge of contemplation. "The Father spoke one Word, which was his Son, and this Word he speaks always in eternal silence, and in silence must it be heard by the soul"[4] (S 100).

Finally, there is one more thing that readers should keep in mind when reading books two and three of the *Ascent*. Namely, that even though John treats of the faculties and the theological virtues separately, they do not function independently or in isolation from one another (cf. A 1. 8. 2; 3. 1. 1). When a person is touched by divine grace, the whole of the soul is affected, not just a part of it; as our faith vision is transformed, so is the object of our hope and our desire or love that seeks to obtain the object that it perceives as its ultimate good.

Visions and Locutions

After John deals with his basic teachings on faith in the first part of book two of the *Ascent,* he treats how the soul should relate to supernatural phenomena such as visions and locutions (chapters sixteen through thirty-two). This section of the *Ascent,* with its seemingly endless categorizing and differentiating the various kinds of visions and spiritual communications, is the one of the driest parts of John writings. Not only does the subject matter seem irrelevant, but John's treatment of the dangers of becoming attached to these phenomena tends to be repetitious.

In spite of this, the reader may glean many insights about the spiritual life from these chapters. Since John is talking about various forms of spiritual experiences, the reader may approach these chapters as an amplification of John's teaching about the dangers and harms of becoming attached to consolation. Ironically, these chapters may prove to be very relevant to any spiritual seeker in our society for they contain a careful analysis of the pitfalls of "seeking an experience" that is so rife in "New Age" spiritualities.

Faith, The Light that Causes Darkness

Faith . . . is a certain and obscure habit of soul. It is an obscure habit because it brings us to believe divinely revealed truths that transcend every natural light and infinitely exceed all human understanding. As a result the excessive light of faith bestowed on a soul is darkness for it; a brighter light will eclipse and suppress a dimmer one. The sun so obscures all other lights that they do not seem to be lights at all when it is shining, and instead of affording vision to the eyes, it overwhelms, blinds and deprives them of vision since its light is excessive and unproportioned to the visual faculty. Similarly, the light of faith in its abundance suppresses and overwhelms that of the intellect. For the intellect, by its own power, extends only to natural knowledge, though it has the potency to be raised to a supernatural act whenever our Lord wishes[5] (A 2. 3. 1).

Why Only the Light of Faith Can Lead Us to God

[F]aith alone . . . is the only proximate and proportionate means to union with God. For the likeness between faith and God is so close that no other difference exists than that between believing in God and seeing him. Just as God is infinite, faith proposes him to us as infinite. . . . Only by means of faith, in divine light exceeding all understanding, does God manifest himself to the soul[6] (A 2. 9. 1).

[Yet] it is noteworthy that among all creatures, both superior and inferior, none bears a likeness to God's being or unites proximately with him. Although truly, as theologians say, all creatures carry with them a certain relation to God and a trace of him (greater or less according to the perfection of being), yet God has no relation or essential likeness to them. Consequently, intellectual comprehension of God through heavenly or earthly creatures is impossible; there is no proportion of likeness[7] (A 2. 8. 3).

Faith, The Darkness that Accesses a Deeper Light

The intellect knows only in a natural way, that is, by means of the senses. If one is to know in this natural way, the phantasms and species of objects will have to be present either in themselves or in their likenesses; otherwise one will be incapable of knowing naturally. . . . If we were told of objects we had never known or seen resemblances of, we would in the end have no more knowledge than before. . . .

If [for example] those born blind were told about the nature of the colors white or yellow, they would understand absolutely nothing no matter how much instruction they received. Since they never saw these colors nor others like them, they would not have the means to form a judgment about them.

Such is faith to the soul; it informs us of matters we have never seen or known, either in themselves or in their likenesses (A 2. 3. 2–3).

Harm that Is Caused from Being Attached to Visions

First, faith will gradually diminish, for sensible experiences detract from it. . . . By not closing the eyes of the soul to all these sensory apprehensions, a person strays from the means of union with God.

Second, if left unrejected these sensory things are an impediment to the spirit because they detain the soul and prevent the spirit from soaring to the invisible.

Third, the soul begins to develop a possessive attitude toward these communications and fails to continue on its journey to genuine renunciation and nakedness of spirit.

Fourth, individuals gradually lose the effect of these communications and the interior spirituality they produce because individuals set their eyes on the sensible aspect, which is the least part of the communications.

Fifth, individuals gradually lose God's favors because they receive these favors as something belonging to themselves. . . . Taking them as one's own and failing to profit by them is the same as desiring to receive them.

Sixth, in desiring to accept them one opens the door to the devil. The devil can then deceive one by other communications expertly feigned and disguised as genuine . . . he can transform himself into an angel of light[8] (A 2. 11. 7).

Divine Communications Only Benefit the Non-possessive Spirit

Obviously, in the measure that individuals divest themselves of willful attachments to the apprehensions . . . these persons will prepare themselves for the goods and communications that are caused by them . . . clarity, freedom of spirit, and simplicity. If the soul desires to feed upon them, the spirit and senses will be so occupied that a free and simple communication of spirituality will be impossible. For, obviously, if it is occupied with the rind, the intellect will have no freedom to receive those spiritual communications (A 2. 16. 11).

Why It Is Not Necessary for the Soul to Pay Attention to Divine Communications in Order to Receive the Grace that They Impart

Such representations and feelings, consequently, must always be rejected. Even though some may be from God, this rejection is no affront to him. Nor will one, by rejecting and not wanting them, fail to receive the effect and fruit God wishes to produce through them.

The reason is that if the corporeal vision or feeling in the senses has a divine origin it produces its effect in the spirit at the very moment of its perception, without allowing any deliberation about wanting or not wanting it. This is likewise so with the more interior communications. Since God grants these favors without the individual's own ability and effort, he causes the desired effect of these favors without this ability and effort since he produces the effect passively in the spirit. The good effect, accordingly, does not depend on one's wanting or not wanting the communication. Were fire to come into immediate contact with a person's flesh, that person's desire not to get burned would hardly be helpful, for the fire produces its effects necessarily. So too with good visions and sensible communications. Even if a person doesn't want them, they produce their effect (A 2. 11. 5–6) (Cf. A 2. 16. 10).

Christ, The Fullness of Revelation

Those who now desire to question God or receive some vision or revelation are guilty not only of foolish behavior but also of offending him by not fixing their eyes entirely on Christ and by living with the desire for some other novelty.

God would answer as follows: If I have already told you all things in my Word, my Son, and if I have no other word, what answer or revelation can I now make that would surpass this? Fasten your eyes on him alone because in him I have spoken and revealed all and in him you will discover even more than you ask or desire. You are making an appeal for locutions and revelations that are incomplete, but if you turn your eyes to him you will find them complete. For he is my entire locution and response, vision and revelation, which I have already spoken, answered, manifested, and revealed to you by giving him to you as a brother, companion, master, ransom, and reward.

If you desire me to answer with a word of comfort, behold my Son subject to me and to others out of love for me, and afflicted, and you will see how much he answers you. If you desire me to declare some secret truths or events to you, fix your eyes only on him and you will discern hidden in him the most secret mysteries, and wisdom, and wonders of God. . . . And if you should seek other divine or corporeal visions and revelations, behold him, become human, and you will find more than you imagine (A 2. 22. 5–6).

Why Does God Give Souls Visions in the First Place?

Since there is so much danger and hindrance to progress in these supernatural visions . . . why does God, who is all wise and in favor of removing obstacles and snares, communicate them?

An answer to this requires the establishment of three fundamental principles. The first comes from Saint Paul's Epistle to the Romans: The works that are done are well-ordered by God (Rom. 13:1).

The second comes from the Holy Spirit in the Book of Wisdom: . . . The Wisdom of God, though she touches from one end to the other (from one extreme to the other), disposes all things gently (Wis. 8:1).

The third comes from the theologians who say: . . . God moves each thing according to its mode.

In order that God lift the soul from the extreme of its low state to the other extreme of the high state of divine union, he must obviously, in view of these fundamental principles, do so with order, gently, and according to the mode of the soul. Since the order followed in the process of knowing involves the forms and images of created things, and since knowledge is acquired through the senses, God, to achieve his work gently and to lift the soul to supreme knowledge, must begin by touching the low state and extreme of the senses. And from there he must gradually bring the soul after its own manner to the other end, spiritual wisdom, which is incomprehensible to the senses. Thus, naturally or supernaturally, he brings people to his supreme spirit by first instructing them through discursive meditation and through forms, images, and sensible means, according to their

own manner of coming to understand. . . . Therefore God
perfects people gradually, according to their human nature, and
proceeds from the lowest and most exterior to the highest and
most interior.

By this method, then, God instructs people and makes them
spiritual. He begins by communicating spiritually to them, in
accord with their littleness or small capacity, through elements
that are exterior, palpable, and accommodated to sense. He does
this so that by means of the rind of those sensible things, in
themselves good, the spirit, making progress in particular acts
and receiving morsels of spiritual communication, may form a
habit in spiritual things and reach the actual substance of spirit,
foreign to all sense. Individuals obtain this only little by little,
after their own manner, and by means of the senses to which
they have always been attached (A 2. 17. 1–5).

Notes

1. Ross Collings, O.C.D., *John of the Cross* (Collegeville, MN: The Liturgical Press, 1990), 104.
2. Thérèse of Lisieux, *Story of a Soul,* trans. John Clarke O.C.D. (Washington, D.C.: ICS Publications, 1976), 179.
3. Collings, *John of the Cross,* 103.
4. For a good treatment of the relationship between contemplation and the articles of faith see Collings, *John of the Cross,* 106–119.
5. We should interpret this passage through the lens of John's teaching that "the intellect must be *perfected* in the darkness of faith" (A 2. 6. 1) (italic added). When John says that the light of faith "overwhelms" the light of the intellect, he is not suggesting that it *destroys* our intellectual powers but rather that faith breaks open and expands them.
6. This passage is based upon the scholastic principle that a means must be proportionate to its end. Applying this principle to the question, "What is the only means that can guide us to God?" John argues that the light of reason is inadequate (is not proportionate) for this task because only God can lead us to God, who communicates his presence to the soul through faith (contemplation).
7. Although John maintains that faith is the only proportionate means that can unite the intellect to God, he does not say that it is the only vehicle

that manifests God's presence to us; creatures as manifestations or "traces" of God's presence is a major theme in *The Spiritual Canticle* (cf. stanzas 4–7).

8. John's teaching in this passage about the damage done by being attached to spiritual communications is identical to his teaching regarding the damage done by being attached to material possessions, etc., namely, that they deprive us of God's spirit, and they engender possessiveness.

The Active Night of the Spirit: Hope

"We are united in the strife that divides us," to paraphrase T. S. Eliot. How true this is when it comes to happiness. We are all united in the same quest, the quest for happiness, but are divided about what happiness consists of. Some seek happiness in wealth, others in fame, and still others in peace of mind. We call the drive that sustains this quest hope, and when hope is transformed by divine grace, it becomes the theological virtue of hope that so orients our lives that we seek happiness in God alone.

For the virtue of hope to grow, says John, the memory has to be purified and transformed because it is the "archives" (A 2. 16. 2) of all of our past experiences that shape our goals in life. To the extent that we choose to dispossess ourselves from seeking things that are not of God, the more we possess God through hope. "In the measure that the memory becomes dispossessed of things, in that measure it will have hope, and the more hope it has the greater will be its union with God" (A 3. 7. 2).

The basic principles regarding the purification of the memory that John deals with in book three of the *Ascent* are applicable to the whole of the spiritual life. He chooses to focus his attention on instructing souls that are growing in contemplation on the importance of detaching themselves from thoughts and images that hinder the soul's reception of the loving knowledge that is being communicated to it.

It is within this context that we must read John's teaching on the purification of memory very carefully. Thus, when he writes of "disencumbering, emptying, and depriving the faculties of their natural authority," it is for a reason: ". . . to make room for the inflow and illumination of the supernatural" (A 3. 2. 2). John is saying that souls that are beginning to experience contemplative prayer must "learn to silence and quiet the faculties so that God may speak" (A 3. 3. 4).

Another aspect of John's teaching on memory that requires careful reading is the nature of the impact that "touches of union" have upon the memory. These intense experiences of God's presence, says John, "empty" and "annihilate" the memory. Such statements can easily convey the erroneous impression that our memories are *erased* in the process of spiritual transformation.

John is not saying this. Rather, he is speaking about a temporary condition in which a soul is unable to *recall* memories because it is so absorbed in God. "Yet once the habit of union . . . is attained one no longer experiences these lapses of memory" (A 3. 2. 8). Grace does not destroy the memory but perfects it; since a soul in union is united to God, it remembers and forgets according to the mind of God (cf. C 26. 16).

John's Audience and Purpose for Writing

[R]eaders must keep in mind the intention we have in writing. Failure to do so will give rise to many doubts about what they read.

Observing how we annihilate the faculties in their operations, it will perhaps seem that we are tearing down rather than building up the way of spiritual exercise. This would be true if our doctrine here were destined merely for beginners who need to prepare themselves by means of these discursive apprehensions. But we are imparting instructions here for advancing in contemplation to union with God. All these sensory means and exercises of the faculties must consequently be left behind and in silence so that God himself may effect divine union in the soul.

This is our task now with the memory. We must draw it away from its natural props and boundaries and raise it above itself (above all distinct knowledge and apprehensible possession) to supreme hope in the incomprehensible God[1] (A 3. 2. 1–3).

The Harm Caused by Not Mortifying the Memory

Spiritual persons who still wish to make use of natural knowledge and discursive reflection in their journey to God . . . are subject to three kinds of harms. . . . Two positive and one privative.

The first . . . involves subjection to many evils arising from this knowledge and reflection, such as falsehoods, imperfections, appetites, judgments, loss of time, and numerous other evils engendering many impurities of soul.

Imperfections meet them at every step, if they turn their memory to objects, to hearing, sight, touch, smell, and taste. By so doing some emotion will cling to them, whether it be sorrow, or fear, or hatred, vain hope, vain joy, or vainglory, and so on. All these are at least imperfections, and sometimes real venial sins.

They subtly contaminate the soul with impurity even when the knowledge and reflection concern God (A 3. 3. 1–3).

The second kind of positive harm possible from knowledge in the memory is due to the devil.

The devil is unable to do anything in the soul save through the operations of its faculties and principally by means of its knowledge, because almost all the activity of the soul's other faculties depends on its knowledge. If the memory is annihilated concerning this knowledge, the devil is powerless, for he finds no means of getting his grip on the soul and consequently can do nothing.[2]

I should like spiritual persons to have full realization of how many evils the devils cause in souls that make much use of their memories; of how much sadness, affliction, vain and evil joy from both spiritual and worldly thoughts these devils occasion[3] (A 3. 4. 1–2).

The third kind of evil engendered by the natural apprehensions of the memory is privative. These apprehensions can be an impediment to moral good and deprive one of spiritual good.

The soul is incapable of truly acquiring control of the passions and restrictions of the inordinate appetites without forgetting and withdrawing from the sources of these emotions. Disturbances never arise in a soul unless through the apprehensions of the memory. When all things are forgotten, nothing disturbs the peace or stirs the appetites. As the saying goes: What the eye doesn't see, the heart doesn't want.

We experience this all the time. We observe that as often as people begin to think about some matter, they are moved and aroused over it, little or much, according to the kind of apprehension. If the apprehension is bothersome and annoying, they feel sadness or hatred, and so on; if agreeable, they experience joy, and so on.[4]

Accordingly, when the apprehension is changed agitation necessarily results. Thus they will sometimes be joyful, at other times sad, now they will feel hatred, now love. And they are unable to persevere in equanimity, the effect of moral tranquility, unless they endeavor to forget all things.

Besides, if souls bestow importance and attention on the apprehensions of the memory, they will find it impossible to remain free for the Incomprehensible who is God (A 3. 5. 1–3).

The Benefits Derived from Mortifying the Memory

From the kinds of harms occasioned by the apprehensions of the memory we can also determine the opposite benefits that come from forgetting them.

In contrast to the first kind of harm, spiritual persons enjoy tranquility and peace of soul due to the absence of the disturbance and change arising from thoughts and ideas in the memory . . . they possess purity of conscience . . . [and] are disposed excellently for human and divine wisdom and virtues.

In contrast to the second, they are freed from many suggestions, temptations, and movements that the devil inserts in souls through their thoughts and ideas.

Contrary to the third kind of harm, the soul is disposed, by means of this recollection and forgetfulness of all things, to be moved by the Holy Spirit and taught by him.

Even though no other benefit would come through this oblivion and void of memory than freedom from afflictions and disturbances, it would be an immense advantage and blessing for a person. For the afflictions and disturbances engendered in a soul through adversities are no help in remedying these adversities; rather, distress and worry ordinarily makes things worse and even do harm to the soul itself[5] (A 3. 6. 1–3).

The Suspension of Memory
that Results from "Touches of Union"

When God on occasion produces these touches of union in the memory . . . the memory is emptied and purged of all knowledge

. . . and remains in oblivion, at times in such great oblivion that it must occasionally force itself and struggle in order to remember something.

Sometimes this forgetfulness of the memory and suspension of the imagination reaches such a degree—because the memory is united with God—that a long time passes without awareness or knowledge of what has happened. . . . These suspensions, it should be noted, occur at the beginning of union and thus are not found in souls who have reached perfection, because the union is then perfect.

Thus in the beginning, when this union is in the process of being perfected, a person cannot but experience great forgetfulness of all things since forms and knowledge are gradually being erased from the memory. Owing to the absorption of the memory in God, a person will show many deficiencies in exterior behavior and customs, forgetting to eat and drink or failing to remember if some task was done, or a particular object seen or something said[6] (A 3. 2. 5–8).

The Memory that Has Been Transformed by Grace

Yet once the habit of union—which is the supreme good—is attained one no longer experiences these lapses of memory in matters concerning the moral and natural life. Rather, such persons will possess greater perfection in actions that are necessary and fitting.

[In union] God now possesses the faculties as their complete lord, because of their transformation in him. And consequently it is he who divinely moves and commands them according to his divine spirit and will. As a result the operations are not different from those of God.

These souls, consequently, perform only fitting and reasonable works, and none that are not so. For God's Spirit makes them know what must be known and ignore what must be ignored, remember what ought to be remembered . . . and forget what ought to be forgotten. . . . Accordingly, all the first movements and operations of these faculties are divine.

Here are some examples of these divine operations. A person will ask a soul in this state for prayers. The soul will not remember to carry out this request through any form or idea of that person remaining in memory. If it is expedient to pray for this one . . . God will move the soul's will and impart a desire to do so.

Another example: At a particular time one will have to attend to a necessary business matter. There will be no remembrance through any form, but, without one's knowing how, the time and suitable way of attending to it will be impressed on the soul without fail[7] (A 3. 2. 8–11).

Notes

1. Just as in regards to book two of the *Ascent,* the reader must keep in mind the overall context of John's instructions on the mortification of the memory; he is speaking about the *active* night. Therefore, John's focus is on the soul's *choices* not to dwell upon the images and apprehensions that the memory presents to the intellect for its consideration.

2. The devil can only influence the intellect and will *indirectly* by means of either sense experiences or images from the memory that he presents to the intellect for its consideration. Therefore, if the soul chooses not to attend to the images that the devil presents, the devil is powerless (cf. N 2. 23).

3. See Teresa of Avila, *The Interior Castle* 2. 1, and *The Way of Perfection,* chapter 39. Also see Ignatius of Loyola, *Rules for the Discernment of Spirits,* esp. no. 315.

4. John's psychology here is akin to the basic premise of modern cognitive psychologists who hold that our feelings are conditioned by our thinking. For a good application of this principle, where John speaks of the importance of controlling the "interior tongue," see the *Precautions* par. 8–9, and the *Counsels,* par. 2–3.

5. Here we have an example of John's common sense advice to his readers: worrying and ruminating about something never helps a situation and often makes it worse. Also see *Ascent* 3. 20. 2, where John talks about the "temporal advantages, prescinding from the spiritual ones" that result from detachment.

6. By means of analogy, the psychodynamics that John is describing are similar to a person who is experiencing severe grief or depression as the result of the loss of a loved one. Just as persons who are suffering severe loss are not present to the external world because they are absorbed in the inner world, so too a soul absorbed in the presence of God is not present to the outer world.

7. In this passage, John is dealing with two of the most important functions of memory that are vital to our identity, remembering and forgetting. Both are necessary in order to function in the world. If we could not remember, we would not be able to recognize the world around us, but if we could not forget, our minds would be deluged in an ocean of images, ideas, and sense impressions. To a certain extent, what we remember and what we forget are linked to the will. We rarely forget what is important to us and tend to forget things that do not hold our interest, or we tend to repress memories that are too painful to bear. Since in the state of union, the soul's will is conformed to God's will, it would follow that what it remembers and what it forgets are according to the will of God.

The Active Night of the Spirit: Love

Because John has often been falsely represented as a grim ascetic, his teaching on human affectivity has frequently been distorted. One of the common misunderstandings of John's doctrine is that the more we grow in holiness, the less human we become. Nothing could be farther from the truth.

In book three of the *Ascent* where John deals with the four natural passions of the will (joy, fear, sorrow, and hope), he does not say that as we grow in holiness that these passions or emotions decrease, but rather as we detach ourselves from seeking our happiness outside of God, they become so ruled by our desire for God, that "a person rejoices only in what is purely for God's honor and glory, hopes for nothing else, feels sorrow only about matters pertaining to this, and fears only God" (A 3. 16. 2).

The passions do not have a pejorative connotation in John's writings; they can be the source of our vices, but they can also give rise to all the virtues. They are like four powerful horses; they can either pull us away from God or toward God; it all depends upon what we are seeking (A 3. 16. 5).

John's treatment of the four passions can be seen as a elaboration of Jesus' teaching "Where your treasure is, there is also your heart," (Mt. 6:21) for what our will is set on obtaining, says John, will determine our emotional reactions. John says that the four passions are like siblings; where one goes the others follow (A 3. 16. 5). In short, they are four interrelated emotional responses to what we seek. For example, if my goal in life (hope) is to become a success in the business world, I will be overjoyed if I succeed, depressed if I fail, and live in fear that my efforts will come to naught.

"Don't aim at success," Viktor Frankl use to admonish his students, "[for] the more you aim at it and make it a target the more you are going to miss it. For success, like happiness, cannot be pursued; it must ensue and it only does so as the unintended side-effect of one's personal dedication to a cause greater than oneself or as the by-product of one's surrender to a person other than oneself. Happiness must happen . . . you have to let it happen by not caring about it."[1] In many ways, this statement of Frankl's sums up the core of John's teaching on love and the purification of the will found in book three of the *Ascent*, namely, that true joy lies in detaching oneself from seeking happiness directly from the things of this world and will only be found as the fruit of dedicating oneself to doing the will of God. Therefore, "The will should rejoice only in what is for the honor and glory of God" (A 3. 17. 2).

The type of joy that John deals with in book three of the *Ascent* is not the natural spontaneous reactions of delight on seeing a beautiful sunset, etc., but what he calls "active joy," the "joy derived from distinct and clear objects, insofar as it is active and voluntary" (A 3. 17. 1). In other words, John is concerned about the satisfaction derived from objects that our will is attached to; for the satisfaction only strengthens the attachment to the object because it is reinforcing.

John deals with six categories of goods in which the will can seek satisfaction or joy (temporal, natural, sensory, moral, supernatural, and spiritual). John spends the greater part of his thesis on love dealing with the harms incurred from being attached to these goods, and the benefits derived from being detached from them. In this section, we will summarize John's treatment on moral goods as representative of his treatment of the other five.

Introduction and Aim of the Thesis on Love

We would achieve nothing by purging the intellect and memory in order to ground them in the virtues of faith and hope had we neglected the purification of the will through charity. . . .

For a treatise on the active night and denudation of this faculty, with the aim of forming and perfecting it in the virtue of the charity of God, I have found no more appropriate passage than the one in chapter six of Deuteronomy . . . *You shall love the Lord, your God, with all your heart, and with all your soul, and with all your strength* [Dt. 6:5]. This passage contains all that spiritual persons must do and all I must teach them here if they are to reach God by union of the will through charity. In it human beings receive the command to employ all the faculties, appetites, operations, and emotions of their soul in God so that they will use all this ability and strength for nothing else (A 3. 16. 1).

The Strength of the Soul Is Ruled by the Will

The strength of the soul comprises the faculties, passions, and appetites. All this strength is ruled by the will. When the will directs these faculties, passions, and appetites toward God, turning away from all that is not God, the soul preserves its strength for God, and comes to love him with all its might.

So a person may do this, we will discuss here purifying the will of all inordinate emotions (A 3. 16. 2).

The Four Passions of the Soul

There are four of these emotions or passions: joy, hope, sorrow, and fear. These passions manifestly keep the strength and ability of the soul for God, and direct it toward him, when they are so ruled that a person rejoices only in what is purely for

God's honor and glory, hopes for nothing else, feels sorrow only about matters pertaining to this, and fears only God. The more people rejoice over something outside God, the less intense will be their joy in God; and the more their hope goes out toward something else, the less there is of it for God; and so forth with all the others. . . .

A person then very easily rejoices in what deserves no rejoicing, hopes for what brings no profit, sorrows over what should perhaps cause rejoicing, and fears where there is no reason for fear (A 3. 16. 2, 4).

Human beings know neither how to rejoice properly nor how to grieve properly, for they do not understand the distance between good and evil (S 63).

The Interconnectedness of the Four Passions

When these emotions go unbridled they are the source of all the vices and imperfections, but when they are put in order and calmed they give rise to all the virtues.

It should be known that, in the measure that one of the passions is regulated according to reason, the others are also. These four passions are so interlinked and brotherly that where one goes actually the others go virtually. If one is recollected actually, the other three in the same measure are recollected virtually. If the will rejoices over something, it must consequently in the same degree hope for it, with the virtual inclusion of sorrow and fear. And in the measure that it loses satisfaction in this object, fear, sorrow, and hope will also be lost. . . .

Where your hope goes, there too will go your joy, fear, and sorrow; and if it turns back, they too will turn back; and so on with each of the other passions.

Accordingly, you should keep in mind that wherever one of these passions goes the entire soul (the will and the other faculties) will also go, and they will live as prisoners of this passion; and the other three passions will be alive in the one so as to afflict the soul with their chains and prevent it from soaring to the liberty and repose of sweet contemplation and union. As a result Boethius claimed that if you desire a clear understanding of the truth, you must cast from yourself joys, hope, fear, and sorrow.[2] As long as these passions reign in the soul they will not allow it to live in the tranquility and peace necessary for the wisdom it can receive naturally and supernaturally (A 3. 16. 5–6).

Joy: The First Emotion of the Will

The first passion of the soul and emotion of the will is joy. Joy . . . is nothing else than a delight of the will in an object esteemed and considered fitting. For the will never rejoices unless in something that is valuable and pleasing to it. We are speaking of active joy, which occurs when a person understands distinctly and clearly the object of its joy and has the power either to rejoice or not.

There is another joy, which is passive. In this kind of joy the will finds itself rejoicing without any clear and distinct understanding of the object of its joy, except at times. It has no power either to possess this joy or not possess it. . . . Our topic now is the joy derived from distinct and clear objects, insofar as it is active and voluntary[3] (A 3. 17. 1).

The Nature of Moral Goods

By moral goods we mean: the virtues and their habits insofar as they are moral; the exercise of any of the virtues; the practice of the works of mercy; the observance of God's law; political prudence, and all the practices of good manners (A 3. 27. 1).

The Two Types of Joy Derived from Moral Goods

When possessed and practiced, these moral goods perhaps merit more joy of will than any of the other three kinds spoken of [temporal, sensory, and natural]. For either of two reasons, or for both together, a person can rejoice in these goods; that is, because of what they are in themselves, or because of the good effected through their instrumentality. . . .

[P]ossessing the three kinds of goods already mentioned deserves no joy of will [for] they neither have any good nor do they produce any in people, because they are perishable and frail. Though they merit some joy for the second reason . . . when people make use of them to go to God, this benefit is so uncertain that, as we commonly observe, a person contracts harm from them more than help.

But even for the first reason (for what they are in themselves), moral goods merit some rejoicing by their possessor. For they bring along with them peace, tranquility, a right and ordered use of reason, and actions resulting from mature deliberation. Humanly speaking, a person cannot have any nobler possession in this life[4] (A 3. 27. 1–2).

Rejoicing in Moral Goods

Because virtues in themselves merit love and esteem from a human viewpoint, and because of their nature and the goods they humanly and temporarily effect, a person can well rejoice in the practice and possession of them. . . .

Though Christians ought to rejoice in the moral goods and works they perform temporally, insofar as these are the cause of the temporal goods we spoke of, they ought not stop there as did the Gentiles, who with the eyes of their soul did not go beyond the things of this mortal life. Since Christians have the light of faith . . . they ought to rejoice in the possession and exercise of these moral goods only and chiefly in the second manner: that insofar as they perform these works for the love of God. . . .

Thus, through their good customs and virtues they should fix their eyes only on the service and honor of God. . . .[5]

They should not set their heart on the pleasure, comfort, savor, and other elements of self-interest these good works and practices usually entail, but recollect their joy in God and desire to serve him through these means (A 3. 27. 3–5).[6]

The Harms that Result from Joy in Moral Goods

Pride

The first is vanity, pride, vainglory, and presumption, for one is unable to rejoice over one's works without esteeming them. This gives rise to boasting (A 3. 28. 2).

Judging and Rivalry

The second is usually linked to the first. It is that people make comparisons judging others to be evil and imperfect, supposing that the deeds and works of others are not as good as their own. Interiorly they have less regard for others, and they sometimes manifest this exteriorly in word (A 3. 28. 3).

Dependence upon Gratification

The third is that since they look for satisfaction in their works, they usually do not perform them unless they see that some gratification or praise will result from them (A 3. 28. 4).

Seeking Joy outside of God

The fourth follows from this third; and it is that they will not find their reward in God since they wished to find, in this life, joy, comfort, honor, or some other thing from their works. . . . Some want praise for their works; others, thanks; others talk about them and are pleased if this person or that or even the whole world knows about them (A 3. 28. 5).

Lack of Perseverance in Virtue

The fifth kind of harm is failure to advance in the way of perfection. As a result of attachment to satisfaction and consolation in their works, some usually become discouraged and lose the spirit of perseverance. . . . For when the occasion of practicing some mortification is presented to these persons, they die to their good works by ceasing to accomplish them, and they lose the spirit of perseverance, which would give them spiritual sweetness and interior consolation (A 3. 28. 7).

Distorted Judgment

The sixth is that they are usually deluded by the thought that the exercises and works that give satisfaction are better than those that do not. And they have praise and esteem for the one kind, but disesteem for the other. Yet those works that usually require more mortification from a person . . . are more acceptable and precious in God's sight because of the self-denial exercised in them, than are those from which one can derive consolation, which very easily leads to self-seeking (A 3. 28. 8).

Incorrigibleness and Growing Cold in Charity

The seventh kind of harm is that human beings, insofar as they do not quell vain joy in their moral deeds, become more incapable of taking counsel and receiving reasonable instructions about the works they ought to do.

Such people become very slack in charity toward God and neighbor, for the self-love contained in their works makes them grow cold in charity[7] (A 3. 28. 9).

The Benefits Derived from
the Removal of Joy from Moral Goods

Freedom from Deception

Great are the benefits derived from restraining the desire for vain rejoicing in this kind of good.

As for the first, the soul is freed from falling into many temptations and deceits of the devil concealed in the joy of these good works. . . . The devil's hidden deceptiveness in this joy is nothing to marvel at because, prescinding from his suggestion, the vain joy is itself a deception, especially when there is some boastfulness of heart over one's works[8] (A 3. 29. 1).

Perseverance in Good Works

The second benefit is a more diligent and precise accomplishment of these works. Such is not the case when one takes pleasure in them with the passion of joy. Through this passion of joy the irascible and concupiscible appetites become so strong that they do not allow leeway for the judgment of reason.[9] As a result people become inconstant in their practice of good works and resolutions; they leave these aside and take up others, starting and stopping without ever finishing anything. Since they are motivated by satisfaction, which is changeable . . . their work ends when the satisfaction does. . . . We can say of those for whom the energy and soul of their work is the joy they find in it that when the joy dies out the good work ceases, and they do not persevere.[10]

Withdrawal of the will from such joy, then, is the cause of perseverance and success. This benefit is great. . . . A wise person is concerned about the substance and benefit of a work, not about the delight and satisfaction in yields. Thus, such a one . . . procures from the work a stable joy without paying the tribute of displeasure (A 3. 29. 2).

Poverty of Spirit

The third is a divine benefit. It is that by extinguishing vain joy in these works a person becomes poor in spirit (A 3. 29. 3).

Steadiness and Stability

The fourth benefit is that those who deny this joy will be meek, humble, and prudent in their work. For they will act neither impetuously and hastily, . . . nor presumptuously, affected by their esteem for the work due to the joy it gives; nor uncautiously, blinded by joy (A 3. 29. 4).

Freedom from the Vices

The fifth benefit is to become pleasing to both God and other human beings and free of spiritual avarice, gluttony, sloth, envy, and a thousand other vices[11] (A 3. 29. 5).

Notes

1. Viktor E. Frankl, *Man's Search for Meaning* (New York: Simon and Schuster, 1984), 13.

2. John refers to this passage from Boethius' work *The Consolation of Philosophy* both here and in the *Ascent* 2. 21. 8. "Rid yourself of joy and fear, put hope to flight, and banish grief. The mind is clouded and bound in chains where these hold sway" (Book 1, 7, translated by V. E. Watts, [London: Penguin Books, 1969], 53). John may have come across this passage in Thomas Aquinas's *Summa theologiae* in which Thomas quotes the first part of the above passage from Boethius when he is dealing with the four principal passions of the soul (I, II, 25, 4). However, another possibility is that John may have derived this quotation from Boethius directly. This author believes that he did. I say this for the following reasons: First, John does not mention Thomas in regards to the four principal passions anywhere in his works. Second, Thomas does not quote the words of Boethius that evoke the prison

symbolism ("bound in chains") that John refers to in the above passage ("afflict the soul with their chains" and "live as prisoners of these passions"). Finally, even though we have no evidence that Boethius' work was a favorite of John's, when we consider that it takes the form of a dialogue between the personification of Philosophy giving advice to the unjustly imprisoned Boethius about keeping perspective while in prison, it is reasonable to assume that Boethius' work may have resonated with John's own prison experience.

3. John may have dealt with the passion of joy first based upon the scholastic principle that anything that is last in the order of execution (the attainment of our goal, which is joy) is first in the order of intention. Again, we see in John's prioritizing the passion of joy, the centrality of desire in his spirituality.

4. Cf. A 3. 20. 2.

5. Cf. A 3. 17. 2.

6. Even though John says that it is permissible for a person to rejoice in moral goods for the temporal advantages that flow from them, he cautions his readers not to seek these advantages as the *motive* for practicing virtue, for we can become just as attached to the consolations of the spirit as we can to the pleasures of the flesh, and "because this harm is spiritual it is particularly ruinous" (A 3. 28. 1).

7. Regarding growing cold in charity as the terminus of our inordinate appetites also see A 1. 10. 4 and A 3. 25. 8.

8. The most characteristic form of deceptiveness employed by the devil is "deceiving them [souls] under the appearance of good rather than of evil. . ." (Pre. *Against the Devil,* par. 10).

9. Scholastic philosophy differentiates the passions or emotions into two groups, the concupiscible or "affective" passions and the irascible or "spirited" passions. The concupiscible emotions consist of three pairs of reactions toward what we perceive as either good or evil: love and hatred, desire and aversion, joy and sadness. The irascible or "spirited" emotions aid us when the good we seek is difficult to attain, or evil difficult to avoid; they consist of five emotions: hope, despair, fear, courage, and anger. Both types of appetites are purified in the dark night. Cf. A 1. 13. 8; N 1. 13. 3; and esp. C 20/21.

10. See the *Counsels* par. 5 and 6 regarding the importance of not setting one's ". . . eyes upon the satisfaction or dissatisfaction of the work at hand as a motive for doing or failing to do it" (par. 5) and its relationship to constancy in the practice of virtue.

11. Cf. N 1. 2–7.

The Passive Night of the Spirit

The purgation of the senses is a prelude to the purgation of the spirit; the night of the senses is comparable to "cutting off a branch"; whereas the night of the spirit is like "pulling up the roots" (N 2. 2. 1). The surgery that takes place in the passive night of the spirit entails the most radical purification possible because the invasion of God's presence into the "substance of the soul," (N 2. 6. 5) lays bear the soul's utter lack of integrity before God. The intensity of the divine light so penetrates the inner recesses of the soul that its darkness is uncovered. As a result of this enlightenment, the soul feels itself "so unclean and wretched that it seems that God is against [it]" (N 2. 5. 5).

The opposite is true; the soul is becoming painfully aware of how much it stands in opposition to God, for grace is exposing the soul's ingrained sinfulness and its deep resistance to God's will. The penetration of God's spirit into the soul not only reveals how "narrow and restricted" (F 1. 23) is its will, but also how tenacious and obstinate are the "vicious darknesses that are contrary to the supernatural light" (F 1. 22). The divine light reveals how strong is the soul's need for control, how mercenary is its love, and how impure are its motives.

The overwhelming feeling of guilt that ensues from this self-knowledge makes the soul feel alienated and isolated not only from God but from others. The mind is so absorbed in the misery that it sees, that the soul feels that its blessings are over forever, and what compounds this suffering is the remembrance of past blessings that stand in stark contrast to its present desolation.

In addition, the loving wisdom of contemplation so incapacitates the mind and heart that the intellect is barren and the emotions stagnate; such souls experience a powerlessness to pray. "They cannot beseech God or raise their minds and affections to him" (N 2. 8. 1). In spite of this void of mind and emotions, the will is focused on God. Just as souls that are being purified in the passive night of sense turn "to God solicitously and with painful care" (N 1. 9. 3), so do souls going through the passive night of the spirit "know that they love God and that they would give a thousand lives for him" (N 2. 7. 7). This is a sign that the suffering that the soul is undergoing is the result of God's purifying presence.

This purification of the spirit is not necessarily continuous, but is often punctuated by periods in which the soul experiences the transformation that is taking place. John compares God with a blacksmith who is working on a piece of iron (soul) (N 2. 10. 6). When the iron is submerged in the forge (contemplation), it experiences all the painful effects of the dark night, but when God withdraws the iron from the fire, the iron glows, that is, the soul feels the love and wisdom that are being enkindled within it.

This metaphor of the iron and the forge and "the burning log" (N 2. 10) are important images in John's writings for they clearly underscore the distinction between the psychological process that is being *experienced* and its underlying spiritual *cause,* which is God's transforming presence.

The Two Purgations

If His Majesty intends to lead the soul on, he does not put it in this dark night of spirit immediately [after] . . . the first purgation and night of sense. Instead, after having emerged from the state of beginners, the soul usually spends many years exercising itself in the state of proficients. In this new state . . . it goes about the things of God with much more freedom and satisfaction of spirit and with more abundant interior delight than it did in the beginning before entering the night of sense. . . . The soul readily finds in its spirit, without the work of meditation, a very serene, loving contemplation and spiritual delight. Nevertheless, the purgation of the soul is not complete. The purgation of the principal part, that of the spirit, is lacking. . . .

The imperfections of these proficients are of two kinds: habitual and actual. The habitual are the imperfect affections and habits still remaining like roots in the spirit, for the sensory purgation could not reach the spirit. The difference between the two purgations is like the difference between pulling up roots and cutting off a branch, rubbing out a fresh stain or an old, deeply embedded one. As we said, the purgation of the senses is only the gate to and the beginning of the contemplation that leads to the purgation of the spirit. . . .

In this purgation [of the spirit], these two portions of the soul [sense and spirit] will undergo complete purification, for one part is never adequately purged without the other. The real purgation of the senses begins with the spirit. Hence the night of the senses . . . should be called a certain reformation and bridling of the appetite rather than a purgation. The reason is that all the imperfections and disorders of the sensory part are rooted in the spirit and from it receive their strength. All good and evil habits reside in the spirit and until these habits are purged, the senses cannot be completely purified of their rebellions and vices. In this night that follows both parts are jointly purified[1] (N 2. 1. 1; 2. 1; 3. 1–2).

Why Contemplation Is a Night for the Soul

Insofar as infused contemplation is loving wisdom of God, it produces two principal effects in the soul; by both purging and illuminating, this contemplation prepares the soul for union with God through love. Hence the same loving wisdom that purges and illumines the blessed spirits purges and illumines the soul here on earth. . . .

Why, if it is a divine light . . . does the soul call it a dark night? In answer to this, there are two reasons this divine wisdom is not only night and darkness for the soul but also affliction and torment. First, because of the height of the divine wisdom that exceeds the abilities of the soul; and on this account the wisdom is dark for the soul. Second, because of the soul's baseness and impurity; and on this account the wisdom is painful, afflictive, and also dark for the soul.

The brighter the light, the more the owl is blinded; and the more one looks at the brilliant sun, the more the sun darkens the faculty of sight, deprives and overwhelms it in its weakness (N 2. 5. 1–3).

Why Divine Wisdom Is Painful to the Unpurified Soul

The Soul's Resistance to Change

[T]his dark contemplation is painful to the soul . . . still unpurged . . . because two contraries cannot coexist in one subject, the soul must necessarily undergo affliction and suffering. Because of the purgation of its imperfections caused by this contemplation, the soul becomes a battlefield in which two contraries combat one another[2] (N 2. 5. 4).

Self Knowledge: The Soul Sees Itself in the Light of God

Because the light and wisdom of this contemplation is very bright and pure, and the soul in which it shines is dark and impure, a person will be deeply afflicted on receiving it. . . . When this pure light strikes in order to expel all impurity, persons feel so unclean and wretched that it seems God is against them and they are against God. . . .

Clearly beholding its impurity by means of this pure light, although in darkness, the soul understands distinctly that it is worthy neither of God nor of any creature. And what most grieves it is that it thinks it will never be worthy, and there are no more blessings for it. . . .

This divine and dark night causes deep immersion of the mind in the knowledge and feeling of one's own miseries and evils; it brings all these miseries into relief (N 2. 5. 5).

Being Undone

The two extremes, divine and human, which are joined here, produce the third kind of pain and affliction the soul suffers at this time. The divine extreme is the purgative contemplation, and the human extreme is the soul, the receiver of this contemplation. Since the divine extreme strikes in order to renew the soul and divinize it . . . it so disentangles and dissolves the spiritual substance . . . that the soul at the sight of its miseries feels that it is melting away and being undone by a cruel spiritual death. It feels as if it were swallowed by a beast and being digested in the dark belly. . . . Because the soul is purified in this forge *like gold in a crucible,* as the wise man says [Wis. 3:6], it feels . . . this terrible undoing[3] (N 2. 6. 1. 6).

A Sense of Powerlessness regarding Prayer

Yet something else grieves and troubles individuals in this state . . . this dark night impedes their faculties and affections, they cannot beseech God or raise their mind and affection to him. It seems as . . . [if] God has placed a cloud in front of the soul so that its prayer might not pass through. . . . And if sometimes the soul does beseech God, it does this with so little strength and fervor that it thinks God does not hear or pay attention to it. . . . Consequently, these persons can neither pray vocally nor be attentive to spiritual matters[4] (N 2. 8. 1).

The Remembrance of Past Graces

To this pain is added the remembrance of past prosperity, because usually persons who enter this night have previously had many consolations in God and rendered him many services. They are now sorrowful in knowing that they are far from such good and can no longer enjoy it[5] (N 2. 7. 1).

A Synopsis of the Dark Night: The Burning Log

For the sake of further clarity in this matter, we ought to note that this purgative and loving knowledge, or divine light we are speaking of, has the same effect on a soul that fire has on a log of wood. The soul is purged and prepared for union with the divine light just as the wood is prepared for transformation into the fire. Fire, when applied to wood, first dehumidifies it, dispelling all moisture and making it give off any water it contains. Then it gradually turns the wood black, makes it dark and ugly, and even causes it to emit a bad odor. By drying out the wood, the fire brings to light and expels all those ugly and dark accidents that are contrary to fire. Finally, by heating and enkindling it from without, the fire transforms the wood into itself and makes it as beautiful as it is itself. Once transformed, the head no longer has any activity or passivity of its own. . . . It possesses the properties and performs the actions of fire.[6]

It is dry and it dries; it is hot and it gives off heat; it is brilliant and it illumines; it is also much lighter in weight than before. It is the fire that produces all these properties in the wood.

Similarly, we should philosophize about this divine, loving fire of contemplation. Before transforming the soul, it purges it of all contrary qualities. It produces blackness and darkness and brings to the fore the soul's ugliness; thus one seems worse than before and unsightly and abominable. This divine purge stirs up all the foul and vicious humors of which the soul was never before aware; never did it realize there was so much evil in itself, since these humors were do deeply rooted. And now that they may be expelled and annihilated they are brought to light and seen clearly through the illumination of this dark light of divine contemplation. Although the soul is no worse than before, either in itself or in its relationship with God, it feels clearly that it is so bad as to be not only unworthy that God see it but deserving of his abhorrence. In fact, it feels that God now does abhor it. This comparison illustrates many of the things we have been saying (N 2. 10. 1–2).

The Forge of God

But sometimes the contemplation shines less forcibly so they may have the opportunity to observe and even rejoice over the work being achieved, for then these good effects are revealed. It is as though one were to stop work and take the iron out of the forge to observe what is being accomplished. Thus the soul is able to perceive the good it was unaware of while the work was proceeding. So too, when the flame stops acting upon the wood, there is a chance to see how much the wood has been enkindled by it (N 2. 10. 6).

The Initial Experiences of the Love and Wisdom that Is Being Infused in the Soul by means of the Dark Night

The Inflaming of the Will

The soul does not always feel this inflaming and anxious longing of love. In the beginning of the spiritual purgation, the divine fire spends itself in drying out and preparing the wood—that is, the soul—rather than in heating it. Yet as time passes and the fire begins to give off heat, the soul usually experiences the burning and warmth of love (N 2. 12. 5).

The Illumination of the Intellect

As the intellect becomes more purged by means of this darkness, it happens sometimes that this mystical and loving theology, [wisdom] besides inflaming the will, also wounds the intellect by illuminating it with some knowledge and light so delightfully and delicately that the will is thereby marvelously enkindled in fervor[7] (N 2. 12. 5).

Notes

1. In N 1. 11. 4 John compares the night of sense to a "narrow gate" or passageway through which we pass in order to journey on the "constricted road," of the night of the spirit.

2. Also see F 1. 22 for John's use of the metaphor of the soul as a battlefield.

3. Words like "disentangles," "swallowed," "dissolves," "melting away," "being undone," "terrible undoing," all suggest that the soul in its imperfect state is like an alloy that has become so fused with things not of God that it has to be "melted down," in order for purification to take place. Cf. N 2, 9, 1.

4. This is one of many places throughout John's writings where he tells us that we should not judge the quality of our prayer based upon our feelings: "many individuals think they are not praying when, indeed, their prayer is deep. Others place high value on their prayer while it amounts to little more than nothing" (A Prol. 6). "Neither the sublime communication nor the sensible awareness of his [God's] nearness is a sure testimony of his gracious presence, nor are dryness and a lack of these a reflection of his absence" (C 1. 3).

5. This suffering echoes a famous line from Boethius' *Consolation of Philosophy*, book 2. 4: "In all adversity of fortune, the most wretched kind is once to have been happy." Dante borrows this line from Boethius and puts it in the mouth of Francesa: "The double grief of a lost bliss is to recall its happy hour in pain" (*Inferno,* canto v. 119) (Ciardi).

6. Cf. F 1. 4. 6. 9.

7. Sometimes God illumines the intellect and inflames the will together and sometimes separately. "All of this is similar to feeling the warmth of fire without seeing its light or seeing the light without feeling the fire's heat. The Lord works in this way because he infuses contemplation as he wills" (N 2. 12. 7). In other words, sometimes we are deeply moved though we know not why, and at other times a deep insight cleaves the mind without necessarily moving the will. These experiences are commonly referred to as divine "touches." Cf. A 2. 24. 4; 26. 3–10; 32. 2–4.

The Light of Early Dawn

John compares the dark night of the soul to the natural night that contains three parts. He likens the night of the senses to "twilight," the time when things begin to fade from sight because the emphasis is on detachment; the night of faith to "midnight" when all is shrouded in darkness, and God who is the goal of the night, is analogous to "the very early dawn just before the break of day" (A 1. 2. 5).

Toward the end of the night of the spirit, God arises in the soul as the light of early dawn. This causes a different type of suffering from that which was predominant in the night of faith. Intense desire to see God is awakened in the soul because by the light of early dawn, God's face is revealed, though not fully. In consequence, the soul longs to gaze upon the beauty of its Beloved of which it has now been given but a glimpse.

The God who *is perceived* and is *still to be revealed,* whom the soul experiences as desire, is the main topic of John's prose work *The Spiritual Canticle.* It is this tension between what is revealed and what is still hidden that "wounds" the Bride with desire for her Beloved. She experiences this wound in the beauty of creation and the loveliness of rational creatures (angels and humans) because as handiworks of her Beloved, she sees in them "a trace of the beauty of her Beloved" (C 6. 1) that "awakens her appetite" (C 6. 4) for a clear vision of her heart's desire. Because the Bride sees the whole of creation in the light of early dawn, it is neither opaque nor transparent, but translucent; she sees her Beloved indistinctly as in a mirror, which makes her desire to see him face to face. This is part of the passive night of the spirit, for the Bride must endure the presence of God who is experienced as absent.

Throughout *The Spiritual Canticle* John employs various images and metaphors of desire, each of which is an expression of God who is simultaneously *always present* and *still yet to come.* Because God is infinite,

125

even for the saints and angels there is still an "infinitude that remains to be understood" (C 7. 9). Thus, for all eternity, we "will forever be receiving new surprises and marveling the more" (C 14/15. 8). Perhaps, it is better to say that the light of early dawn does not "wound us" but lays bear the wound that *we are,* creatures made in the image and likeness of God whose desire will forever unfold in joyful anticipation of the God who is and who is to come.

The Bride's Complaint

In this first stanza the soul, enamored of the Word, her Bride-groom, the Son of God, longs for union with him through clear and essential vision. She records her longings of love and complains to him of his absence, especially since his love wounds her. Through this love she went out from all creatures and from herself (C 1. 2).

Pierced by Love

The pain and sorrow I ordinarily suffer in your absence was not enough for me, but having inflicted on me a deeper wound of love with your arrow, and increasing my desire to see you, you flee as swiftly as the stag and not let yourself be captured even for a moment. . . . He [God] bestows these [visits] to wound more than heal and afflict more than satisfy, since they serve to quicken the knowledge and increase the appetite (consequently the sorrow and longing) to see God [1] (C 1. 16. 19).

What We Long for Is in the Longing

She calls her desires, affections, and moanings "shepherds," because they pasture the soul with spiritual goods—a shepherd or pastor is one who feeds or pastures—and by means of these yearnings God communicates himself to her and gives her the divine pasture. Without them he communicates little to her[2] (C 2. 1).

The Wound

God created all things with remarkable ease and brevity, and in them he left some trace of who he is . . . endowing them with innumerable graces and qualities. . . . Through them one can track down his grandeur, might, wisdom, and other divine attributes (C 5. 1, 3).

The soul, wounded with love through a trace of the beauty of her Beloved, which she has known through creatures, . . . [is] anxious to see the invisible beauty that caused this visible beauty. . . .

Since creatures gave the soul signs of her Beloved and showed within themselves traces of his beauty and excellence love grew in her and, consequently sorrow at his absence. . . .[3] Every glimpse of the Beloved received through knowledge or feeling or any other communication (which is like a messenger bringing the soul news of who he is) further increases and awakens her appetite, like the crumbs given to someone who is famished. . . .

How well you know my Spouse, that [these] messengers [your creatures] augment the sorrow of one who grieves over your absence: first, through knowledge they enlarge the wound: second, they seem to postpone your coming. . . . You have revealed yourself to me as through fissures in a rock (C 6, 1. 2. 4. 6).

The Sore Wound

In the previous stanza the soul showed her sickness, or wound of love for her Bridegroom, caused by the knowledge irrational creatures gave to her. In this stanza she asserts that she is wounded with love because of another higher knowledge she receives of her Beloved through rational creatures (angels and humans), creatures more noble than the others. She also asserts that she is not merely wounded, but is dying of love. This dying of love is due to an admirable immensity these creatures disclose to her, yet do not completely disclose. Because this immensity is indescribable she calls it an "I-don't-know-what."

. . . [T]hese rational creatures cause two kinds of suffering of love in her, the sore wound and death; the sore wound because . . . they relate a thousand graces of the Beloved . . . death, from what . . . lies "behind their stammerings."

. . . Besides the fact that these creatures wound me with a thousand graceful things they explain about you, there is a certain "I-don't-know-what" that one feels is yet to be said, something unknown still to be spoken, and a sublime trace of God as yet uninvestigated but revealed . . . that cannot be put into words[4] (C 7. 1. 5. 9).

Impregnated by One's Beloved

How do you endure
O life, not living where you live,
and being brought near death
by the arrows you receive
from that which you conceive of
your Beloved? (stanza 8).

In this stanza she [the Bride] addresses her own life, stressing the grief it causes her. The meaning of the stanza is: Life of my soul, how can you endure in this bodily life, for it is death to you and privation of that true spiritual life of God, in which through essence, love, and desire you live more truly than in the body?

To understand these lines it should be known that the soul lives where she loves more than in the body it animates; for she does not live in the body, but rather gives life to the body and lives through love in the object of her love.

Moreover, how can you endure in the body, since the touches of love (indicated by the arrows) that the Beloved causes in your heart are enough to take away your life? These touches so impregnate the soul and heart with the knowledge and love of God that she can truthfully say she conceives of God[5] (C 8. 2–4).

The Boundless Ocean of God

Sometimes God favors advanced souls through what they hear, see, or understand—and sometimes independently of this—with a sublime knowledge by which they receive an understanding or experience of the height and grandeur of God. Their experience of God in this favor is so lofty that they understand clearly that everything remains to be understood.

One of the outstanding favors God grants briefly in this life is an understanding and experience of himself so lucid and lofty that one comes to know clearly that God cannot be completely understood or experienced. This understanding is somewhat like that of the Blessed in heaven: Those who understand God more understand more distinctly the infinitude that remains to be understood; those who see less of him do not realize so clearly what remains to be seen (C 7. 9).

It is no wonder that God is strange to humans who have not seen him, since he is also strange to the holy angels and to the blessed. For the angels and the blessed are incapable of seeing him fully, nor will they ever be capable of doing so . . . they will forever be receiving new surprises and marveling the more[6] (C 14, 15. 8).

Notes

1. This is an expression of one of John's main teachings about our desire for God; it detaches us from desires contrary to God's will. "A more intense enkindling of another, better love (love of the soul's Bridegroom) is necessary for the vanquishing of the appetites . . ." (A 1. 14. 2). In the above passage, this enkindling is felt as sorrow because God is experienced as absent,

and like the sorrow of mourning, the longing for one's Beloved so absorbs the soul that it becomes detached from other things. The "arrows" or "touches" or "wounds" of love may be compared to those moments of piercing remembrance that a person experiences during a grieving process.

2. John is saying that the soul's longing for God whom she feels is absent is actually an experience of God who is present.

3. John rightly connects an experience of beauty with sorrow. Jacques Maritain says that every experience of beauty is always silhouetted by sorrow. He writes: ". . . [B]eauty does not mean merely perfection. . . . [For] anything 'totally perfect' on earth . . . lacks that longing and 'irritated melancholy' . . . which is essential to beauty here below. . . . A totally perfect finite thing is untrue to the transcendental nature of beauty. And nothing is more precious than a certain sacred weakness . . . through which infinity wounds the finite." *Creative Intuition in Art and Poetry* (New York: Meridan Books, 1955), 127–8.

4. Since the Bride is living in the light of God's dawn, creation has become more translucent or sacramental. The beauty of nature is evocative of God who is "infinitely elegant," (A 1. 4. 4) and the goodness and kindness of human beings sorely wounds the soul for they are foretastes of the eternal love of God.

5. This passage conveys the image of a women whose lover is dead, but she is pregnant with his child. The child of her womb is simultaneously an intimate experience of his presence and a constant reminder of his absence.

6. These passages are based upon the doctrine of the incomprehensibility of God, who will remain incomprehensible for all eternity and the eternal expansion of the soul into God. Thus, the beatific vision is no static reality but an endless unfolding of the Being of God. As Gregory of Nyssa writes, "The soul will never attain completion because it will never reach its limit. . . . Since God of his nature is boundless, communion of nature with him must be boundless and always capable of receiving more." Ladislaus Boros, *Open Spirit*, trans. Erika Young (New York: Paulist Press, 1974), 105.

On the Threshold of Eternity

In *The Living Flame of Love* and the latter part of *The Spiritual Canticle* (stanzas 22–40), John deals with the life of a soul that is united with God by love. To express the oneness of life shared in this union, John, like many mystics before him, uses the metaphor of marriage.

In marriage or any human relationship in which two people have grown old together in love, they have come to know one another so intimately that they share one mind and heart between them; they know what the other person is thinking and feeling and have come to see the world through the eyes of the other. The same is true for the soul united with God in love; because it shares the very life of God, "all the acts of the soul are divine" (F 1. 4).

The metamorphosis of psyche and spirit that result from this process of deification is so radical that readers may think that John's descriptions of them are hyperboles or poetic license, but John tells us that the opposite is true, that his words fall short of the reality that they attempt to express.[1] He says that no one, "not even they who receive these communications," has the ability to adequately express the graces given to them. Yet, in spite of the poverty of language, "*something* of their experience overflows in figures, comparisons and similitudes, and from the abundance of their spirit pours out secrets and mysteries" (C Prol. 1) (italic added).

This union that John speaks of is of two kinds: *habitual union* and *actual union*. Habitual union is the transformed state of the soul united with God; John compares it to the glowing embers of a log that has been transformed into fire (F 1. 16). The substance of the soul and its faculties are so drenched with divine life that they can say with Saint Paul, "It is no longer I that live but Christ that lives within me" (Gal. 2:20). The soul has so taken on the mind and heart of Christ that "it no longer understands by means of its natural vigor and light, but by means of . . . divine wisdom"; it is so "united with the divine love, [that it loves] with the strength and purity of the Holy Spirit" and "the memory [is] changed into eternal apprehensions of glory" (N 2. 4. 2). All of these transformations occur because "the intellect of this soul is God's intellect; its will is God's will; its memory the memory of God; and its delight is God's delight" (F 2. 34). These are some of the main features of habitual union, which is the most important type of union for John; it is what the soul *has become*: "it has become God through participation" (F 2. 34).

This transformation of the soul that fills it with "the utter fulness of God," (Eph. 3:19) manifests itself in various ways: there is a freedom from fear of what other people think (C 28. 7); a stable peace that issues from the quelling of the passions (C 20/21, 35); an ability to find joy in the good of others (C 22); an alacrity of response in doing God's will (C 28. 5); the ability to extract spiritual profit from every circumstance (C 27. 8), and the recovery of innocence (C 26. 14–15), to name a few.

These manifestations of habitual union may be compared to some of the habitual qualities that characterize the day to day relationship of a couple who have grown old together in love; there is harmony and peace between them; they find joy in one another's presence; they joyfully respond in love to the needs of the other, etc.

Actual union, on the other hand, may be compared to those intense moments of intimacy between a couple who have grown in love together; for example, the moment of orgasm, when an utter sense of oneness with one's beloved is experienced in the feeling of having been dissolved and fused with the other, or moments of overwhelming gratitude that overcome a person at the realization of the great treasure that he or she has in his or her partner.

Similarly, experiences of actual union are intense visitations of God's presence that a soul experiences *within* the state of habitual union. John uses various metaphors to explain the difference between habitual and actual union. For example, he compares the graces of actual union to flames of fire that flare up from the glowing embers of habitual union. Or he says that habitual union is like resting in a "sweet embrace" (F 4. 14) on the breast of one's beloved "in immense tranquility" (F 4. 15) while he is asleep, and actual union is like those moments when he awakens.

John calls these intense encounters with God in actual union "awakenings" (F 4) or "touches" (F 2). These "awakenings" or "touches" are of

many kinds.[2] They can be moments of profound awareness and penetrating insight when there is an "immersion of the soul in wisdom" (F 1.
17). Such experiences can take the form of a deep realization of the
meaning of life or a panoramic vision of how divine providence has
shaped one's history. I believe that C. S. Lewis touches on such an experience at the end of *The Screwtape Letters*. At the moment of death, Lewis's
protagonist has a vision of how various saints and angels have accompanied him on his life's journey.

> . . . when he saw them he knew that he had always
> known them and realized what part each one of them had
> played at many an hour in his life when he had supposed
> himself to be alone, so that now he could say to them, one by
> one, not "Who *are* you?" but "So it was *you* all the time." All
> that they were and said at this meeting woke memories. The
> dim consciousness of friends about him which had haunted
> his solitudes from infancy was now at last explained; that
> central music in every pure experience which had always
> just evaded memory was now at last recovered.[3]

This haunting passage, I believe, captures an experience that arises out
of a memory that has been "changed into eternal apprehensions of
glory," (N 2. 4. 2) that has become "the memory of God" (F 2. 34). For
memory is not a mere recording of past events, but an interpretation of
them. Thus, the memory, transformed by grace, views its life in the light
of divine providence. When recording the story of her soul, Saint
Thérèse wrote:

> It is not, then, my life properly so called that I am going
> to write: it is my *thoughts* on the graces God deigned to grant
> me. I find myself at a period in my life when I can cast a
> glance upon the past; my soul has matured in the crucible of
> exterior and interior trials. And now, like a flower strength-
> ened by the storm, I can raise my head and see the words of
> Psalm 22 realized in me: "The Lord is my Shepherd. . . . To
> me the Lord has always been merciful and good. . . ."[4]

An "awakening" of memory we may compare to an intense realization
of how God has shepherded one's life in mercy and love.

Other examples of "awakenings" are unitive experiences of the interre-
latedness of all things in God in which "the soul is conscious of how all
creatures, earthly and heavenly, have their life . . . in him [God] . . ." (F

4. 5), and become "for the soul a harmonious symphony of sublime music surpassing all concerts and melodies of the world" (C 14, 15. 25).

As the Bride awakens to the immense beauty of God, she simultaneously awakens to her own beauty, for the ravishing face of her Beloved is a mirror reflecting her own countenance. And what is even more marvelous than this is that because she shares the very life of God, her face mirrors back to her Beloved his own countenance, so that, "each looking at the other may see in the other their own beauty . . ." (C 36. 5). As the Bride begins to grow in the capacity to look into the eyes of her Beloved, she discovers a wonderful thing: that just as her beauty is a reflection of God's, so too is her desire.

The first part of *The Spiritual Canticle* records the longings of the Bride for her Beloved, but beginning with stanza twenty-two, where John first deals with the effects of full union, the Bride discovers that her desire for her Beloved is but a dim reflection of her Beloved's desire for her: "it should be known that if anyone is seeking God, the Beloved is seeking that person much more" (F 3. 28).

This is a joyous "awakening" for the Bride, to know that she can make her Beloved happy, for between two people who deeply love one another, to be able to give joy to one's Beloved is the greatest of joys. This is why "The soul's aim is a love equal to God's. She always desired this equality, naturally and supernaturally, for lovers cannot be satisfied without feeling that they love as much as they are loved" (C 38. 3). And this is what union accomplishes, for "the soul loves God with the will and strength of God himself," and " . . . God makes her love him with the very strength with which he loves her" (C 38. 3. 4).

The love story of the Bride and her Beloved that we find throughout John's writings is an ancient story of desire; it is the story of the god Eros who fell in love with a mortal named Psyche (soul), made her his Bride and raised her up to be a goddess.

Alacrity of Response

All this energy [of the soul] is occupied in God and so directed to him that even without advertence all of its parts, . . . are inclined from their first movements to work in and for God. The intellect, will, and memory go out immediately toward God; and the affections, senses, desires, appetites, hope, joy, and all the energy from the first instant incline toward God. . . . As a result she frequently works for God, and is occupied in him and his affairs, without thinking or being aware that she is doing so. . . .

[T]he soul in this state of spiritual espousal ordinarily walks in the union of love of God, which is a habitual and loving attentiveness of the will to God[5] (C 28. 5. 10).

Being Settled in God, the Soul No Longer Looks for Its Peace outside Itself.

Occupied in God Alone

Before reaching this gift of surrender of herself and her energy to the Beloved, the soul usually has many unprofitable occupations by which she endeavors to serve her own appetite and that of others. For we can say she had as much work as she had many habitual imperfections. These habitual imperfections can be, for example, the trait or "work" of speaking about useless things, thinking about them, and also carrying them out, not making use of such actions in accord with the demands of perfection. She usually has desires to serve the appetites of others, which she does through ostentation, compliments, flattery, human respect, the effort to impress and please people by her actions, and many other useless things. In this fashion she strives to please people, employing for them all her care, desires, work and finally energy.

She says she no longer has all this "work" because all her words, thoughts, and works are of God and are directed toward him without any of the former imperfections[6] (C 28. 7).

The very pure spirit does not bother about the regard of others or human respect, but communes inwardly with God, alone and in solitude as to all forms, and with delightful tranquility, for the knowledge of God is received in divine silence (S 28).

Finding a Home in God

The Bridegroom continues the explanation of this happiness over the blessing the Bride has obtained through the solitude in which she formerly desired to live. This blessing is a stable peace and unchanging good. When the soul has become established in the quietude of solitary love of her Bridegroom . . . she is settled in God and God in her. . . .

The solitude in which she lived [before she was united to God] consisted of the desire to go without the things of the world for her Bridegroom's sake. . . . She formerly practiced this solitude, in which she lived, in trial and anguish because she was imperfect, but now she has built her nest in it and has found refreshment and repose in having acquired it perfectly in God. . . . The soul has found a place in God where she can satisfy her appetites and faculties[7] (C 35. 1. 4).

The Harmony of Creation

Silent Music, Sounding Solitude

In that nocturnal tranquility and silence and in the knowledge of the divine light the soul becomes aware of Wisdom's wonderful harmony and sequence in the variety of her creatures and works. Each of them is endowed with a certain likeness of God and in its own way gives voice to what God is in it. So creatures will be for the soul a harmonious symphony of sublime music surpassing all concerts and melodies of the world. She calls this music "silent" because it is tranquil and quiet knowledge without the sound of voices. And thus there is in it the sweetness of music and the quietude of silence. Accordingly, she says that her Beloved is silent music because in him she knows and enjoys this symphony of spiritual music. Not only is he silent music, but he is also sounding solitude.

This is almost identical with silent music, for even though that music is silent to the natural senses and faculties, it is sounding solitude for the spiritual faculties. When these spiritual faculties are alone and empty of all natural forms and apprehensions, they can receive in a most sonorous way the spiritual sound of the excellence of God, in himself and in his creatures. . . . In this same way the soul perceives in that tranquil wisdom that all creatures, higher and lower ones alike, according to what each in itself has received from God, raise their voice in testimony to what God is. She beholds that each in its own way, bearing God within itself according to its capacity, magnifies God. And thus all these voices form one voice of music praising the grandeur, wisdom, and wonderful knowledge of God (C.14, 15. 25–27).

The Interconnectedness of All Creation in God

In this awakening they [all created things] not only seem to move, but they all likewise disclose the beauties of their being, power, loveliness, and graces, and the root of their duration and life. For the soul is conscious of how all creatures, earthly and heavenly, have their life, duration, and strength in him. . . .

And here is the remarkable delight of this awakening: The soul knows creatures through God and not God through creatures. This amounts to knowing the effects through their cause and not the cause through its effects. . . . [T]he soul [is] awakened from the sleep of natural vision to supernatural vision. . . . And the soul sees what God is in himself and what he is in his creatures in only one view, just as one who is opening the door of a palace beholds in one act the eminence of the person who dwells inside together with what that sovereign is doing. . . . [W]hat I understand about how God effects this awakening and view given to the soul . . . is that he removes some of the many veils and curtains hanging in front of it so that it might get a glimmer of him as he is. . . .

What a person knows and experiences of God in this awakening is entirely beyond words. Since this awakening is the communication of God's excellence to the substance of the soul[8] (F 4. 5–7, 10).

The Revelation of the Soul's Goodness and Beauty

The soul, then, conscious of the abundance of its enrichment, at the time of these glorious encounters feels to be almost at the point of departing for complete and perfect possession of its kingdom, for it knows that it is pure, rich, full of virtues, and prepared for such a kingdom. God permits it in this state to see its beauty, and he entrusts to it the gifts and virtues he has bestowed; for everything is converted into love and praises, and it has no touch of presumption or vanity since it no longer bears the leaven of imperfection that corrupts the mass (F 1, 31).

Yet were we to desire to speak of the glorious illumination he [God] sometimes gives to the soul in this habitual embrace, which is a certain spiritual turning toward her in which he bestows the vision and enjoyment of this whole abyss of riches and delight he has placed within her, our words would fail to explain anything about it. As the sun shining brightly on the sea lights up great depths and caverns and reveals pearls and rich veins of gold and other minerals, and so on, the Bridegroom, the divine sun, in turning to the Bride so reveals her riches that even the angels marvel and utter those words of the Song of Songs: *Who is she that comes forth like the morning rising, beautiful as the moon, resplendent as the sun, terrible as the armies set in array?* [Sg. 6:10]. In spite of the excellence of this illumination, it gives no increase to the soul; it only brings to light what was previously possessed so she may have the enjoyment of it (C 20, 21. 14).

The Restoration of Innocence
and the Capacity to Rejoice in the Goodness of Others

The Restoration of Innocence

In a way, the soul in this state resembles Adam in the state of
innocence, who did not know evil. For she is so innocent that she
does not understand evil, nor does she judge anything in a bad
light . . . since she does not have within herself the habit of evil by
which to judge them. . . . This is characteristic of God's spirit in
the soul: He gives her an immediate inclination toward ignoring
and not desiring knowledge of the affairs of others, especially
that which brings her no benefit (C 26. 14–15).

Rejoicing in the Good Fortune of Others[9]

The soul that has reached this state of perfection is not content
with extolling and praising the excellence of her Beloved, the
Son of God, or of telling in song and rendering thanks for the
favors she receives from him and the delights she enjoys in him;
for she makes references also to those he bestows on other souls.
In this blessed union of love she is aware of both[10] (C 25. 1).

The Ability to Derive Spiritual Nourishment
from Every Situation

[T]he soul that has reached this state of spiritual espousal
knows how to do nothing else than love. . . .
She does this not merely because he [the Bridegroom] desires
it, but also because the love by which she is united to him moves
her to the love of God in and through all things. Like the bee that
sucks honey from all the wildflowers and will not use them for
anything else, the soul easily extracts the sweetness of love from

all the things that happen to her; that is, she loves God in them. Thus everything leads her to love[11] (C 27. 8).

A Generative Love

The interior acts he [the Holy Spirit] produces [in the soul] shoot up flames, for they are acts of inflamed love, in which the will of the soul united with that flame, made one with it, loves most sublimely. Thus these acts of love are most precious; one of them is more meritorious and valuable than all the deeds a person may have performed in the whole of life without this transformation, however great they may have been. . . .

[A]ll the acts of the soul [in this state] are divine, since both the movement to these acts and their execution stem from God[12] (F. 1, 3–4).

God's Desire for the Soul

Great was the desire of the Bridegroom to free and ransom his Bride completely from the hands of sensuality and the devil. Like the good shepherd rejoicing and holding on his shoulders the lost sheep for which he had searched along many winding paths [Lk. 15:4–5], and like the woman who, having lit the candle and hunted through her whole house for the lost drachma, holding it up in her hands with gladness and calling her friends and neighbors to come and celebrate, saying rejoice with me, and so on [Lk. 15:8–9], now, too, that the soul is liberated, this loving Shepherd and Bridegroom rejoices. And it is wonderful to see his pleasure in carrying the rescued, perfected soul on his shoulders, held there by his hands in this desired union (C 22. 1).

In the first place it should be known that if anyone is seeking God, the Beloved is seeking that person much more[13] (F 3. 28).

The Breathing of God

This breathing of the air is an ability that the soul states God will give her there in the communication of the Holy Spirit. By his divine breath-like spiration, the Holy Spirit elevates the soul sublimely and informs her and makes her capable of breathing in God the same spiration of love that the Father breathes in the Son and the Son in the Father. This spiration of love is the Holy Spirit himself, who in the Father and the Son breathes out to her in this transformation in order to unite her to himself. There would not be a true and total transformation if the soul were not transformed in the three Persons of the Most Holy Trinity in an open and manifest degree.

And this kind of spiration of the Holy Spirit in the soul, by which God transforms her into himself, is so sublime, delicate, and deep a delight that mortal tongue finds it indescribable, nor can the human intellect, as such, in any way grasp it . . . for the soul united and transformed in God breathes out in God to God the very divine spiration that God . . . breathes out in himself to her.

In the transformation that the soul possesses in this life, the same spiration passes from God to the soul and from the soul to God with notable frequency and blissful love. . . .

One should not think it impossible that the soul be capable of so sublime an activity as this breathing in God through participation as God breathes in her. For, granted that God favors her by union with the Most Blessed Trinity, in which she becomes deiform and God through participation, how could it be incredible that she also understand, know, and love—or better than this be done in her—in the Trinity, together with it, as does the Trinity itself[14] (C 39. 3–4)!

Notes

1. In realizing that it is difficult, if not impossible, to imagine beyond our own experience, John writes: "Since these rare experiences . . . are more remarkable than credible, I do not doubt that some persons, not understanding them through their own knowledge or knowing of them through experience, will either fail to believe them or consider the account an exaggeration; or they will think these experiences less than what they really are" (F 1. 15).

2. "There are many kinds of awakenings that God effects in the soul, so many that we would never finish explaining them all" (F 4. 4). Thus, the examples that John gives should not be considered to be an exhaustive list of the mystical experiences that a soul can experience in union.

3. C. S. Lewis, *The Screwtape Letters and Screwtape Proposes a Toast* (New York: The Macmillan Company, 1961), 147–8.

4. Thérèse of Lisieux, *Story of a Soul*, trans, John Clarke O.C.D. (Washington, D.C.: ICS Publications, 1976), 15.

5. Being "occupied in God" does not mean that a soul in union is oblivious or inattentive to others; just the opposite is true; because it is occupied in loving God, it is attentive to its neighbor. Saint Teresa writes regarding a soul in union: "You may think that as a result the soul will be outside itself and so absorbed that it will be unable to be occupied with anything else. On the contrary, the soul is much more occupied than before with everything pertaining to the service of God." Teresa of Avila, *Interior Castle,* VII, 1, 8, p. 430.

6. Saint Teresa in speaking of souls whose love is perfect writes: "[T]hey laugh at themselves because of the affliction they once suffered as to whether or not their love was repaid." Teresa of Avila *The Way of Perfection,* in *The Collected Works of St. Teresa of Avila,* vol. 2. trans. Otilio Rodriguez O.C.D. and Kieran Kavanaugh O.C.D. (Washington, D.C.: ICS Publications, 1980), chap. 6, par. 7, p. 64.

7. What John means by solitude in this passage is singleness of heart; it refers to the soul that loves God alone. It is the solitude of detachment. In this passage, John uses the word solitude or detachment in two ways. First, he refers to the solitude of the "active night," those *choices* that we make in order to detach ourselves from things so that we can make room for God in our hearts: "by striving for perfection . . . [she] formerly practiced this solitude." Second, John speaks of the solitude that is the *consequence* of these choices; the detached and empty heart has not become a void but a "nest," "a place in God" where the soul "attains to complete refreshment and rest. . . ." Throughout John's writings, the process of detachment is presented in a positive light because he connects it to the peace and inner harmony that it brings to the soul. Even in chapter thirteen of the first book of the *Ascent,* that stark chapter in which John outlines his program for morti-

fication, he underlines this fact. "In this nakedness the spirit finds its quietude and rest. For in coveting nothing, nothing tires it by pulling it up and nothing oppresses it by pushing it down, because it is in the center of its humility. When it covets something, by this very fact it tires itself" (A 1. 13. 13). Cf. A 3. 20. 2; Pre 1; Co 1; S 79, 118, 132.

8. In the above two selections, John is dealing with what spiritual authors call the "spiritual senses" of the soul. The "spiritual senses" is a metaphorical way of speaking of the deepest capacity of the soul (the substance of the soul) to perceive and experience spiritual reality. "By the 'feeling' of the soul, the verse refers to the power and strength the substance of the soul has for feeling and enjoying the objects of the spiritual faculties; through these faculties a person tastes the wisdom and love and communication of God. The soul calls these three faculties (memory, intellect, and will) 'the deep caverns of feeling' because through them and in them it deeply experiences and enjoys the grandeurs of God's wisdom and excellence" (F 3. 69). Thus, when the mystics speak of seeing God with the "eyes of the soul" (C 10. 4), or having a "palate bathed in glory" (F 1) or feeling the "delicate touch" of God, even though they are using symbolic language, they are referring to real ways or modes or textures of experiencing spiritual reality.

However, it should also be mentioned that even though the language of the "spiritual senses" should not be taken literally, neither should it be considered as merely metaphorical, because since the human person, according to John, is a unity of "sense" and "spirit," when the spirit is purified and transformed by grace, it has a certain impact upon the bodily senses. How to express this change in bodily perception is a challenge. Broadly speaking, however, John tells us that the unpossessive heart has the capacity to *enjoy* the world around it more than a possessive one, because it *perceives* things according to their inner reality (substance) (A 3. 20. 2). The poet Rilke perhaps put it best when he said, "Not till it is held in your renouncing is it truly there."

9. This is one of the great blessings and sources of joy (and relief) that flow from union with God. When a soul can find happiness in the blessings of others, not only can it find joy in all things, but it is also relieved of the burden of fear and sadness that ensue from envy and competitiveness.

10. Throughout his works, John draws attention to the interrelationship between ourselves, others, and God. For example, when a "beginner" is puffed up with pride, he is envious of and threatened by the spiritual progress of others, judges them severely and in his arrogance is "more daring with God than proper" (N 1. 12. 3). Conversely, when God places the "beginner" in the dark night, the searing light of contemplation humbles him with self knowledge, which in turn makes him less self righteous toward his neighbor and begins to "commune with God more respectfully and courteously" (N 1. 12. 3). Similarly, as a soul in union begins to see its own beauty and goodness reflected in the beauty and goodness of God, it is able to perceive the beauty and goodness of others.

11. John is speaking of part of the genius of the saints who knew how to find spiritual profit in every situation, even the most painful. This is an expression of the work of contemplation (God's presence) "that teaches the soul secretly and instructs it in the perfection of love . . ." (N 2. 5. 1). Thérèse writes: "Your Thérèse is not in the heights at this moment, but Jesus is teaching her to learn 'to draw profit from everything, *from the good* and *the bad* she finds in herself.'" Thérèse of Lisieux, *Letters of St. Thérèse of Lisieux: Volume II 1890–1897,* trans. John Clarke O.C.D. (Washington, D.C.: ICS Publications, 1988), 795. Saint Francis de Sales in speaking of a soul that possesses the true love of God (devotion), uses the same metaphor of the bee that John uses. "Look at the bees upon the thyme; they find there a very bitter juice but in sucking it they turn it into honey. It is true the devout find mortification bitter in itself, yet they convert this bitterness into sweetness when they practice it." Francis de Sales, *Introduction to the Devout Life,* trans. Michael Day (Wheathampstead, Hertfordshire: Anthony Clarke, 1990), pt. I, chap. 2, p. 9.

12. At the end of the *Ascent,* John makes a similar connection between the depths of a person's spiritual life and the effectiveness of their preaching. "[P]reaching is more a spiritual practice than a vocal one . . . [for] it has no force or efficacy save from the interior spirit. . . . Although it is true that good style, gestures, [etc.] are more moving and productive of effect when accompanied by this good spirit, yet without it the sermon imparts little or no devotion to the will even though it may be delightful and pleasing to the senses and the intellect" (A 3. 45. 2. 4).

13. Graham Greene once said that we never get accustomed to being less important to people than they are to us. This is especially true between lovers; not to be desired by one's lover as much as one desires him or her is a deep wound. At the beginning of *The Spiritual Canticle,* it was the Bride who desires and seeks out her evasive lover, but at the beginning of stanza twenty-two, the real situation is revealed; it is the Bridegroom who desires and seeks the Bride; the desire of the Bride for her Beloved is a dim reflection of his desire for her.

In the literature of western mysticism, the mystics speak of a truth that sounds almost blasphemous, namely, that God desires us and "needs" to be united to us in order to be completely happy. Denys Turner points out that the mystics speak of a certain mutuality of desire between God and the soul. This teaching that God is both "Yearning and Love" (*The Divine Names,* 712 C) is found throughout the writing of Pseudo Dionysius, whose writing greatly influenced John of the Cross. See Denys Turner, *Eros and Allegory: Medieval Exegesis of the Song of Songs* (Kalamazoo, Michigan-Spencer, Massachusetts: Cisterian Publications, 1995), esp. 47–68.

14. Cf. F 4. 16. As John approaches the end of *The Spiritual Canticle* and attempts to express the utter oneness of a soul with God that exists in union, he compares it to the intimacy and unity that exists among the three Persons of the Trinity by means of the mutual "spiration" or breathing between the Father and the Son, "the Father breathes in the Son and the Son

in the Father." And his mutual giving and receiving (inhaling and exhaling so to speak) *is* the love that is the bond between them that we call the Holy Spirit.

This pure requited love, this reciprocal surrender within the Trinity is mirrored in all creation. D'Arcy writes: "The simplest statement of the law which governs what is highest and lowest in the Universe can be called that of 'Give and Take.' In the most elementary changes in the physical world there is gain and loss, the taking on of something and the passing on of what once was and no longer is. Aristotle describes such change in terms of matter and form, where there is always something determinable which is made determined and something which actively determines, and gives it form. Something seems to slide away into nothingness itself while being at the same time a provider of what is to come, and something enters into possession . . . one gives the other takes. The giving is a surrender and implies a certain passivity, perhaps even unto death and extinction. The desire which is felt by the two parties in this momentary or prolonged union accords with the role played. There is a whoop of triumph, the exultant mastery in the act of possession, and on the other side, there is a joy in self-surrender even to absorption and total extinction in the other. . . . The important fact to notice is the universal fact of duality. . . . Now, whereas in nature these [two] instincts go their own way, careless often of individual life, on a human level each self must grow in the taking and giving and each is a sacred life which must be respected. . . . Every human person has these two loves within him. . . . [T]his law of the two [types of love] in one, of giving and taking, is to be found in its primordial and perfect expression in God himself, where in the mutual love of the Trinity all is given without loss and all is taken without change, save that a new Person is revealed in this wondrous intercommunion who is love itself." M. C. D'Arcy, *The Mind and Heart of Love* (Cleveland: The World Publishing Company, 1956), 14–16.

What D'Arcy is intimating is that the "give and take" of love is the dual dynamic of our deepest instinct for relationality that defines what it means to be human, for it is a participation in the very life of God. Just as in Trinitarian theology, it is not said that the Father has a relationship to the Son but *is* a relationship to the Son, and the Son does not have a relationship to the Father but *is* a relationship to the Father. So too, as creatures *creatio ex nihilo*, our entire being is *received* from God, and yearns to *return* to God in joyful thanksgiving. This is the drama of the universe. Thomas Aquinas describes creation as an *exitus* or "going forth" from God, and redemption as a *reditus* or "return to God." "The flowing forth of God" says Ruysbroeck, "always demands a flowing back; for God is a Sea."

The mystics stretched language to its breaking point to try to express this "give and take," this mutual act of surrender that has come to full consciousness between God and the soul in union. Ruysbroeck cries out, "To eat and to be eaten! This is Union!" The savage intensity of this image of consuming and being consumed by one's Beloved speaks of the desire to completely absorb and to be absorbed in the other. Or in the act of love we desire to be both inside our lover and to have our lover inside of us; we want to hold and be held, to contain and be contained, to succor and to be nourished, to give and to receive.

Likewise, the metaphor of inhaling and exhaling is a symbol of mutual self surrender, and John's final metaphor for the life-giving stance of non-possessive love, for we can only live by breathing and if we hold on to our breath we die. "Deny your desires and you will find what your heart longs for" (S 15). Detachment in John's writings is letting go of all that keeps us unconscious of who we are. We are "asleep in God's presence," (F 4. 8) and when we awake, we will discover that we have always been resting in the "intimate embrace" (F 4. 14) of our Beloved.

Chronology

1529   Marriage of John's parents, Gonzalo de Yepes and Catalina Alvarez in Fontiveros.

1530   Birth of Francisco their first son.

1531–40 Birth of Luis their second son; year uncertain.

1542   John is born (Juan de Yepes).

1545   John's father Don Gonzalo dies.

1546   John's mother Catalina goes to Toledo with her three children to seek assistance from Gonzalo's family. Catalina's brother-in-law agrees to raise Francisco as a son, but because Francisco receives abusive treatment from his aunt, Catalina brings him back to Fontiveros.

1547   Luis dies.

1548–51 The Yepes family moves to Arevalo to better their living conditions; Francisco marries Ana Izquierdo.

1551   The family moves to Medina del Campo to secure more work.

1551–58 John attends the School of Doctrine.

1556–7 At the invitation of Don Alonso Alvarez John begins to work as an orderly in a hospital for people who have contracted sexually communicable diseases.

1559–63 John studies the humanities at the Jesuit college in Medina.

1563   John enters the Carmelite novitiate in Medina and makes his profession of vows the following year.

1564–68 John studies theology at the University of Salamanca.

1567   John is ordained to the priesthood and, while home at Medina, meets Teresa who convinces John to help her in the work of her reform.

1568   The first house of Discalced friars is established in Duruelo; John is appointed novice master and subprior.

1571   John becomes the rector of the Carmelite house of studies at Alcalá.

1572   John becomes the confessor to Carmelite nuns at the convent of the Incarnation in Avila at the request of Teresa.

1577   John is abducted by the Calced Carmelites and brought to Toledo where he is imprisoned for nine months.

1578   John escapes from his Toledo prison, remains hidden in the Carmelite convent of nuns of Toledo for a period of time, and, when his health returns, travels to the Discalced chapter being held in Almodóvar, where he is elected vicar of the monastery in El Calvario.

1579   John becomes the founder of the Carmelite college in Baeza and serves as the prior there until 1582.

1580   Catalina, John's mother, dies.

1582   John is elected prior of Los Mártires in Granada and serves in this capacity until 1588.

1588   John travels to Madrid, attends the first General Chapter of the Carmelite Reform and is elected First Definitor and prior of the monastery in Segovia.

1591   John moves to La Peñuela to prepare for departure to the missions in Mexico but becomes sick and is transferred to Ubeda for medical assistance. On 14 December, John dies.

1675   John is beatified by Clement X on 22 January.

1726   John is canonized on 26 December by Benedict XIII.

1926   John is declared a universal Doctor of the Church by Pius XI on 24 August.